*the exciting story
of the life of*

Hudson Taylor

*founder of the
China Inland Mission*

*written by
Catherine Mackenzie*

*Published by
Christian Focus Publications*

This book is dedicated
to three missionaries.

Three women who lived for Christ.

Meg Byers
Annie Macangus
and Dolly Mackenzie.

They never travelled
to the other end of the globe
but their influence
for the cause of Christ
is far reaching.

I thank God for each of them.

I thank my God every time
I remember you.

Philippians 1:3

The author would like to take this
opportunity to thank the following people
who made the publication of this book
possible.

Mark Ellis and the OMF team
Thank you for your cooperation and for
providing the maps. Also thank you for
writing the chapter
'A New Adventure'.
It has been great working with you
on this project.

Marianne Ross and Jason Ross
Thank you for your hard work and
enthusiasm.

The team at Christian Focus Publications
Thank you for waiting,
encouraging and praying!

Rachael Phillips
Thank you for doing the cover for this
book - against all the odds
and glandular fever!

Well done all of you!

Important note: The following book on Hudson Taylor makes use of material written by Hudson Taylor. There are fictional journal entries, dialogue and day to day occurrences which hopefully will make this book easier to read. Hudson and Amelia did go on excursions to Lunn Woods. This particular entry pp32-35 is true to life but fictional. Other minor occurrences follow the same pattern throughout the book but on the whole this book is biographical. Should reading this book make you wish to go on and read a complete biography about Hudson Taylor and read the letters and journals he and his family actually wrote so much the better. I recommend the following titles: *Hudson and Maria* written by John Pollock, published by Christian Focus Publications and *A Man in Christ*, by Roger Steer, published by OMF Books.

© 1999 Catherine Mackenzie
ISBN 1-85792-423-1
reprinted 1999

Published by Christian Focus Publications Ltd
Geanies House, Fearn ,Tain, Ross-shire, IV20 1TW,
Scotland, Great Britain

Cover Illustration by Rachael Phillips

Printed and Bound in Great Britain by Cox and Wyman

TIME LINE

1832	Born, Barnsley, England.
1849	Becomes a Christian at seventeen years old. Is called to China.
1851	Works as doctor's assistant in Hull.
1852	Begins medical training in London. Nearly dies of malignant fever.
1853	Sails for China as agent of Chinese Evangelisation Society.
1854	Settles in Shanghai.
1855	First Chinese convert.
1856	Begins work in Shantou. Moves to Ningpo.
1857	Resigns from CES. Begins a relation ship with Maria Dyer.
1858	Marries Maria Dyer.
1860-61	Returns to England due to illness. Edits a new version of the Chinese New Testament.
1862	Qualifies as a member of the Royal College of Surgeons; passes his midwifery examinations.
1865	Writes *China: Its Spiritual Need and Claims*.
1865	On Brighton Beach prays for twenty-four missionaries to accompany him back to China. China Inland Mission begins.
1866	Returns to China.

1867	Hudson's daughter, Grace Taylor dies of meningitis, aged eight.
1868	Work begins at Yangzhou. Yangzhou riots.
1870	Maria dies, aged thirty-three.
1871	Hudson returns to England and marries Jennie Faulding.
1872	Returns to China with Jennie.
1874	Hudson seriously injures his back. Returns to England and directs the mission from his bed.
1881	CIM now has ninety-six missionaries; one hundred Chinese assistants; seventy tations.
1887	102 candidates join CIM.
1895	1153 workers since 1889 appeal
1900	Boxer Massacres. CIM loses fifty-eight missionaries and twenty-one children.
1904	Jennie dies of cancer.
1905	Hudson Taylor dies.
1949-52	All CIM missionaries forced to leave China. CIM renamed OMF (Overseas Missionary Fellowship)
1965	OMF celebrates centennial.
1990	OMF 125th anniversary.
1995	OMF becomes OMF International.

Maps
of
China

Yangzhou
Shanghai
Ningbo
Ganzhou
Shantou

Yangtze River

1000 miles
1500 kilometres

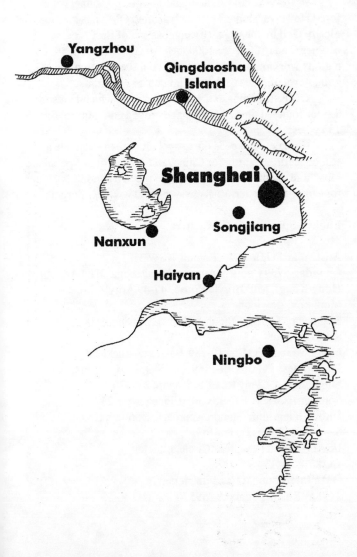

O M F

In 1949-52, all China Inland Mission personnel were forced to leave China. The newly named OMF has a vision to glorify God by the urgent evangelisation of East Asia's peoples. Today there are 1000 members of OMF from 30 nations working throughout East Asia, seeking to bring the good news of Jesus to those who don't know him.

OMF still holds to the principles with which Hudson Taylor founded the CIM. We have proved God faithful over 135 years.

China today needs the gospel more than ever. We are still concerned to pray for China, and can introduce people to jobs there. Contact us if you want to receive a monthly 'Pray for China' newsletter. Visit our website at www.omf.org.uk

English-Speaking OMF Centres

Australia: PO Box 849, Epping, NSW 2121
Canada: 5759 Coopers Avenue, Mississauga ON, L4Z 1R9
Hong Kong: 15/F Argyle House, 47-49 Argyle Street, Mongkok, Kowloon
Malaysia: 3A Jalan Nipah, off Jalan Ampang, 55000, Kuala Lumpur
New Zealand: PO Box 10-159, Balmoral, Auckland
Philippines: PO Box 10-1159, QCCPO, 110 Quezon City
Singapore: 2 Cluny Road, Singapore 259570
Southern Africa: P O Box 3080, Pinegowrie, 2123
United Kingdom: Station Approach, Borough Green, Sevenoaks, Kent, TN15 8BG
USA: 10 West Dry Creek Circle, Littleton, CO 80120-4413
OMF International Headquarters:
2 Cluny Road, Singapore 259570

Contents

The Adventure begins

There is a saying that 'mad dogs and Englishmen go out in the midday sun'. The sweltering heat of the Chinese sun sent most foreigners scurrying for the shade and a cool bath, but not all.

'Foreign Devil! Foreign Devil!' The shouts echoed down the busy Chinese street where crowds of people spilled out from tall houses and broken down huts. Scruffy children ran from their play to see the commotion. Some stared unabashed at the strange foreigner making his way down the road. Others were frightened and hid behind the skirts of older sisters or mothers.

Ornate Chinese temples and strong stalwart city walls belied the extreme poverty of the majority of these Shanghai residents. Poverty was a daily reality for many.

'Foreign Devil!' The cry got louder. 'Here he comes, with his silly yellow hair and skin the colour of goats milk. Look at his eyes as bright as a flower. It's strange to see so many colours on one person.' Old grandmothers and young women took great delight in discussing every inch of the peculiar foreigner. 'Look at the silly buttons on his front and his back. Why does he have buttons on the front of his clothes and then buttons on the back as well?'

Chinese people wore simple loose fitting clothes but the foreigners wore fussy, complicated clothes which made no sense. Chinese men wore their hair in pigtails down the back of their heads. The rest of the head was then shorn. This foreigner had hair like straw all over his head.

Young men followed the yellow haired foreigner a few strides behind. They carried large baskets on long bamboo poles. These baskets held a variety of different products ready for selling at one of the many Shanghai markets. One man held one end of the pole and another held the opposite end with the large heavy basket swaying in between. They sniggered at the strange man until he felt embarrassed and awkward. He looked at his clothes and at the other people round about. He too could see that everybody was staring at him. In his hand he carried a large book and a few pages of notes. 'He is heading towards the town meeting place', said one grandmother. 'He must have important news to tell.'

Scrawny old chickens were kicked out of the way and babies were slung onto backs as the locals followed the pale faced foreigner.

Women walked awkwardly on tiny bound feet. This was because little girls all over China were taken aside by their parents at quite an early age to have their feet bound in tight bandages. This stopped their feet from growing and meant that when they were older they would have tiny, dainty feet which the Chinese loved. No woman with great big feet could expect to get a husband. Men didn't like big feet. Big feet were considered unattractive. As well as that, if you had a wife with small feet, it meant that she couldn't run very far or very fast without getting caught. Women were not allowed to make their own choices or live their own lives. They were caught in a system which, at best treated them like second class citizens, and at worst mistreated them and made their lives miserable.

More voices joined in the babble of sound, 'Here he comes, here he comes - the "Foreign Devil" in his funny clothes!' Men, women, children, dogs and one or two braying donkeys added to the chaos. The young stranger coughed awkwardly as he was still conscious of all the amusement his clothing was causing. The young men and women, the farmers and merchants, the young children and babies all stared at him. A drop of sweat dripped from the end of his nose. With a white handkerchief he wiped the sweat away and caused more amusement.

'Ha ha! Look at him he wipes his face with a big white flag. It is even whiter than his face!' He coughed again and prayed earnestly that these people would not waste time laughing at him but would listen to what God was saying.

When he began to speak, the crowd were surprised. The slim pink lips spoke good Chinese.

'I want to tell you about the one true God. He is the one who made heaven and earth and who has made you! My name is Hudson Taylor and I have travelled a very long way to come and tell you that the one true God loves you and wants you to love him. I tell you the truth.'

A Chinese merchant stood at the edge of the crowd, curious about all the goings on. 'He says that he will tell the truth? I have heard of these foreign barbarians. They come from far beyond the middle kingdom where the uncivilised people live. They are uneducated and have no manners. I wonder why all these people listen to him?'

The young Chinese merchant laid down the cotton he had taken to sell at the market that day and listened to what this barbarian had to say.

The barbarian now raised his voice to make himself heard above the noise of the crowd.

'The God who created the heavens, and the earth, who created the great Yangtze river that flows by us, does not want us to live without hope. He wants to forgive us our sins. He wants us to come back to him and to live our lives with him. But God must punish sin! So he sent his son, Jesus Christ to live on this earth. Jesus didn't sin. He was perfect. He came to earth as a little child. He lived a perfect life. He healed the sick, made the lame walk and raised the dead to life. He lived a perfect life instead of us, then he died instead of us. Our wickedness deserves God's anger and because of our sin we deserve to die. But Jesus Christ died so that we might live and three days later he came back to life! Death did not defeat him.'

Gasps of astonishment and disbelief went up from all corners. The Chinese merchant stood, thoughtfully, his hand on his chin. There was truth here. He could feel it. No other religion had touched his heart in the way that this Jesus did. The merchant had tried many religions, including Buddhism. This Jesus Christ was different. He was truth. The foreigner shouted out above the babble 'If you believe and trust in Christ you will live for ever with him. But if you don't believe in Christ when you die you will face eternal punishment.'

The crowd 'oohed' and 'aahed' at this amazing speech. Some laughed at the 'silly foreigner' and his 'silly story'.

The Chinese merchant picked up the cotton and left without saying a word. But as he walked he spoke for the first time with the one who had laid down his life for him on a cross.

The young missionary, Hudson Taylor, sighed as he watched the man disappear round the corner.

The merchant turned for one last look at the heavy black suit, and the sandy coloured hair and wondered, 'Who is this Hudson Taylor and why does he come to this town?'

Barnsley Beginnings

Hudson Taylor's journey to China began almost from the day he was born, if not before. His physical journey to China, however, began in September 1853. That night a wind was howling round the house, rattling down chimney pots and chasing draughts all around the old Yorkshire chemist's. This was where the Taylor family lived. Hudson slept soundly in his own bed, snoring, beneath the heavy quilt. A quiet, gentle, face with lilac eyes peered round the door. Hudson's mother whispered, 'Shhh, child. Sleep well.' Softly she shut the door and padded her way down the corridor. 'I still call him child even though he's wearing long trousers, has had a broken engagement and is off to the other side of the world.'

Mrs Taylor shivered as the wind whipped around her ankles, 'Well, at least I have him at home, but for how long?' She resisted the temptation to rush back into his room and sweep his untidy blond curls away from his forehead. It was hard to think of someone leaving her whom she loved so completely. It wasn't Hull this time or London - in a matter of weeks her child would be on a ship headed for China. Despite Mr Taylor's reassurances that China was in fact a very civilised country with an intelligent people, she got a lump in her throat every time she thought of her young son living there, on his own.

Tiptoeing silently she entered her bedroom to the gentle snores of her husband. Instead of going to bed Mrs Taylor sat, perched, on the window seat, with a shawl wrapped round her shoulders. Mr Taylor snored on. His wife sighed, 'He always finds sleep so easy.' A sudden draught snuffed the candle out. She quickly rose to light it again - there was only one way she would sleep tonight. Soon Mrs Taylor snuggled back into the cushions, wrapped herself in a thick blanket and began to write.

She remembered the strict rules she had given the children in the past. 'No reading at bed time.' The very thought that they might set their bed clothes alight with a fallen candle was reason enough to ban reading in bed. But here she was just writing her journal at midnight! Well, it would give her peace of mind. The journal though old and faded was a record of her thoughts and prayers, hopes and dreams. Thankfully communication with God didn't insist upon pen and paper, but writing down her concerns and memories gave her something to look back on.

'It is amazing,' she thought 'how much I can thank God for. Just reading through all these old journals really shows me how much God has looked after us all.' A moonbeam caught her eye. 'There was a moon just like that on the night that James first plucked up the courage to walk me home.'

She looked over at the now old James Taylor. As he breathed in and out his long whiskers rose up and down in between the snores. Mrs Taylor smiled at her husband, looked at the moon, blazing through their bedroom window and remembered that first walk home. She smiled as she wrote...

I was quite struck with the young James Taylor but never thought he would feel the same way. Then all of a sudden he came up to me and said:

'Miss Hudson. You sang beautifully tonight.'

I was only sixteen years old, the daughter of a Methodist minister and had such a sweet, sweet voice that everyone referred to me as 'The Nightingale'. That evening I had sung a medley of hymns and spiritual songs for a select gathering of friends. My father was the local minister and everyone loved to hear his young daughter sing.

'They call you "The Nightingale" don't they? I can see why!' James blushed underneath his new moustache. He was only seventeen years old and it had taken him months to pluck up the courage to speak to me. Now I thought he was going to ruin everything by getting all shy and rushing frantically out the door. But no! I smiled at him beguilingly and he smiled back. Maybe things weren't so bad after all.

James squeaked, 'May I walk you home?' Coughing, he added in a slightly deeper voice, 'It would be my pleasure.'

Dazed, and hardly believing my luck, I nodded demurely. I was a young governess to a local family, he was an apprentice in the town of Rotherham. He was also a hard worker. Both of our families approved of the union. So one thing led to another and seven years later in April 1831 we were married. Now, here we are, at 21 Cheapside, Barnsley. I'm a lot older with a few wrinkles round the eyes. I'm not quite so neat and trim as I was then. No one calls me 'The Nightingale' any more.

Mrs Taylor sighed and rose from her bed to get another glass of water.

I am so thankful James and I are united in our faith. It makes things so much easier. We are at one where it really matters. God is first before anything.

I could have married a man who didn't love Christ. But what would that have been like? I shiver at the thought that I might have been stuck in a marriage where Christ wasn't present.

Lord, a marriage without you is second best. But I thank you that you have given me the best. Your love is the best love. Your love is so much stronger than any other love.

I remember those first few months together where it was still such a novelty to wake up and just be together. What precious times we had with our Lord and his word. Each morning was like a search for what God was going to say to us for that day. And the Lord never failed us. His word was always direct to our hearts, to our lives. I remember one morning in particular. The Bible lay open at Exodus and James was avidly pointing at this verse then another.

'Read Exodus chapter thirteen and some of these chapters in Numbers. Do you see? "Sanctify unto me all the first born'', "All the first born are mine.''''

I followed his finger, reading each verse in turn. What was James trying to say?

Pulling myself out of the chair I tried to get comfy. This first pregnancy was really tiring me. I couldn't sit long in the one spot and was bothered with sickness almost continuously. Tired and irritable I must have looked quite stern and apologised to James for being so grumpy.

'I'm just a bit uncomfortable. These seats are so hard.'

Waddling over to the window I thought to myself 'Oh, baby! Come on. What is keeping you?' Supporting myself against the windowsill I looked at the passing world outside, and sighed, 'But James, what do you mean by setting apart children to the Lord. We don't have any child to set apart yet.'

'Yes we do.' James looked me in the face. 'He or she is waiting to come into this world and what better welcome to have than to be given to God. Given into his care.'

I suddenly felt a little heel or fist stretching and bumping into my side. Give up our little son or daughter before we had even seen each other. The thought was incredible!

'James how can I? I don't want to give our baby away.'

'I know. I know. All I can do is let you think over this yourself. It's not easy and maybe you feel it's unnecessary. Just take some time. I'll be in the store if you need me. I know you love this baby. Just think, what better way to show your love than by giving the child to a God who is love? His love is so deep. You can't possibly love this child more than God already does.'

I nodded, despite my doubts, smiled and then stared out the window again. James left me to think. Grimacing I sat down again on the dining-room chair and leafed through the verses once more. 'What does it mean to give this baby to you God? Why do you want the first-born in particular? I suppose it glorifies you when I trust you in this special way with my first child. I pray that my child will glorify you, Lord Jesus, by living for you and serving you. Lord, my main purpose in life is to glorify you and enjoy you for ever.' I took a deep breath and made a decision there and then. 'Lord, God, I am ready now to give my child completely to you. You have asked for the firstborn. I give you all my children. I give you this family, all our futures, all our lives.'

I breathed a sigh of relief. 'That's better!' Then Baby kicked me. 'Hello there little one. You've been set apart today! You have been given to God the Almighty. You're quite safe.' I smiled at where I thought the baby might be. Perhaps even now the little child was starting to wonder what all these sounds and movements were in that strange place he or she couldn't understand. I whispered excitedly, 'You've been set apart for a great God. I know he will do great things with you!' Easing myself up out of the uncomfortable chair I made my way through to the store room. 'James will we pray now?'

James dusted his hands down his overall and hugged me. 'Yes!' The father-to-be grinned widely.

The noise of gentle movements from the girl's room next door gently woke Mrs Taylor. Stretching herself she smiled at the memories and dreams of last night. Gone was dream of being a young expectant mother. Gone was the dream of holding a new born baby boy in her arms. May 21, 1832 was a fond but distant memory. Hudson Taylor was now a young man and no longer her little boy. Other memories came to mind too. Memories of her young son, William, who had died before he was eight years old. Memories of watching and praying over all her young children. William and Hudson had been very close as children. Hudson still missed him. However, now he had a special bond with his sisters, particularly with his sister Amelia. The bond between Hudson and Amelia was so strong it almost excluded everybody else. Mrs Taylor watched her oldest daughter as she grew up. Amelia was daily discovering new things about her world and herself. Hudson too had come on in leaps and bounds lately. All her youngsters were stretching their wings. Louisa, the youngest in the family, was particularly interested in being independent. She always voiced her opinions and insisted on making up her own mind. She stubbornly refused to be forced into anything she didn't agree with. She was the only member of their family who was not a believer. Mrs Taylor and the others were worried about Louisa but there was no hurrying her. Mrs Taylor knew that Louisa would always make her own decisions, in her own time. She just prayed that God would take a hand in the whole situation and bring this young, free-spirited creature to himself, soon.

Mrs Taylor was glad that her oldest daughter, Amelia, had come to Christ early. It was so good how they were now not just mother and daughter but sisters in the Lord Jesus Christ and really good friends. None of her children were perfect. They all had faults and imperfections. Louisa was headstrong. Hudson could be too. He was also a hopeless romantic and could fall in love at the drop of a hat. Amelia was possessive, particularly of Hudson and Mrs Taylor sometimes saw how that possessiveness caused problems between Amelia and Louisa. The problems were nothing major and were probably normal problems for any family as close as theirs.

As the family rose, to wash away the sleep from their eyes, Mrs Taylor had to leave her memories and begin to get ready for another day. This morning's reality was breakfast to cook and sleepy heads to waken up. She walked briskly down the corridor, stopping briefly to sweep the untidy curls from off Hudson's sleepy face. 'Hudson Taylor,' she whispered in his ear. 'It's time for breakfast.'

'Mmmm,' Hudson mumbled. 'Sausages?'

***

Breakfast was soon over and Mrs Taylor sat down to enjoy some peace and quiet. Mr Taylor had gone through to the front of the house which was the chemist's. Hudson and his sister Amelia wandered off down the road chatting animatedly. Hudson had asked Louisa to come but she had remained behind and was now up in her room tidying out a closet and rearranging stuff. Perhaps Amelia and Louisa had had another quarrel? Between sips of the steaming hot tea Mrs Taylor worried about her youngsters, especially young Amelia and Louisa. They appeared to be squabbling a bit lately. 'Amelia has always been a bit possessive of Hudson, Lord. Hudson doesn't seem to see the tension between his two sisters, but I see it quite clearly sometimes. They try to hide it but they forget how well I know them. I can spot a problem or a difficulty a mile off, especially when one of my children is involved. Amelia and Louisa are probably feeling the strain more now. They are both starting to worry about Hudson's departure.' She carefully laid the delicate china cup in its saucer and savouring the pleasure of a few moments to herself she picked up her journal once more.

This morning I remembered seeing a mop of sandy hair bobbing up and down on top of Amelia's bed.

It was late on a bright summer's evening. Amelia just could not sleep and Hudson had the 'bright' idea about telling her a story. However, it soon became clear that this was not the type of story to send one to sleep. Hudson shouted out '...the highwayman came riding, lashing his whip in the air as his poor old horse struggled to flee the oncoming cavaliers. He whipped her and whipped her as they fled into the night.

'Over the stile they jumped.' (Hudson jumped too sending the bedspread flying.)

'Over the stone-dyke they leapt!' (A pillow hit the floor.)

'A wide swirling river lay ahead' (Hudson waved the bed sheet in the air for effect) 'But the river was too wide for the old horse to swim. What would they do now? The highwayman lashed his whip once again into the poor horse's flank. Just then the horse reared and sent the wicked old highwayman - splat into the dark, foaming depths - and with a kick of her hind legs, and a swish of her long tail she vanished into the night - free at last!'

It was quite a story - even I felt relieved that the poor old horse had made her bid for freedom.

Hudson has many gifts from you Lord. The other night he had played his flute at the family musical evening. It was as if I too had been swept away by his music to a place of peace and rest. But even then there have been times when I have worried about him, about his strength of mind, which he could so easily waste and squander. I remember an evening when we were in church. It was so cold. We all huddled into the family pew and tried to keep warm. But Hudson had his mind focused on a pew near the front. I cast a sideways glance at him. 'What is he up to?' I wondered.

Dame Margaret Lawrence, a local country lady, with more ancestors than is probably decent, kept jumping in her seat and turning round to look straight at Hudson. She did it several times. She was beginning to look very annoyed and just a bit bewildered. Then Hudson got bored and his concentration wandered elsewhere.

James told me later that it's a 'Taylor Talent'. He said to me, 'When we put our minds to it we Taylors can almost will anyone to do anything. Just like Hudson tonight. He willed the old Dame to turn round and look at him. He knows if he puts his mind to it he can make people do silly things like that. It's just a game to him. But don't worry my dear. I will talk with Hudson and advise him to stop.' Thankfully he did.

Mrs Taylor pondered before continuing to write. It was amazing what she still discovered about her family even after all these years.

Time after time I have sat in this room and wondered exactly how well do I know my family, how well do I know my own son. There's not a year goes past when I don't discover something new about each of them. But, Lord God, Heavenly Father, our times are in your hands and you know every hidden corner of our beings. There is nothing we can hide from your penetrating gaze. You know me better than I know myself and even your love is greater than anything that comes out of my cramped and tiny heart. You love my children too. I don't understand why you let little William die. I don't always understand why Hudson has to go to China. God, I am sorry when I don't trust you in the way that I should.

Mrs Taylor stopped to look at the clock. 'Where has the time gone? There's darning to do.' The demands of a family were ever present.

Hurriedly she put the journal away and brought out the darning basket. With precise neat stitching she started to mend a pile of socks and shirts. Mrs Taylor was no stranger to hard work. She sang quietly as she brought the needle in and out.

***

The clock struck twelve as the two wanderers returned from their fresh air and exercise. Amelia laughed at one of Hudson's jokes and Louisa crept down the stairs to join them. Mrs Taylor looked at her three youngsters as she quickly laid the table. 'Lunch will be ready soon. Amelia, can you help me in the kitchen? Louisa has helped all morning. It's now her turn for relaxation.' Amelia blushed as she followed her mother into the kitchen. Louisa and Hudson sat together in the parlour where Hudson shared the joke. Amelia looked at her mother, feeling slightly anxious.

'You've done all the work, Mother. What do you really want to say?'

'I just want to remind you, Amelia, that as well as a very worthy brother you have a young, slightly flighty little sister, who I know prattles on a bit and does silly things, but who is really quite hurt when you don't include her.'

'Mother, Hudson asked her to come this morning but she didn't want to.'

'Hudson asked her. You didn't. And, in case you hadn't noticed, the problem isn't Hudson, it's you.'

A tear pricked the daughter's eye and the mother's heart felt for her. Hugging her close she whispered, 'If the problem is with you the solution is with you. All you need is prayer, perseverance - and a little bit of compassion.'

Amelia hugged her mother back. To herself she

admitted that she was jealous of any time Louisa spent with Hudson. For too long Amelia had been possessive of her brother to the exclusion of Louisa. Fighting back the tears she apologised, 'I am sorry mother, I have been wrong. Instead of squabbling with Louisa I should have been loving her. Instead of keeping Hudson to myself I should have spent time with Louisa too. I will try.'

Mrs Taylor turned to look at her young daughter, 'Remember your sister Louisa has still not made her peace with God. Do not squabble or hurt her unnecessarily. Love your little sister into the Kingdom of God. Pray for her continuously. You prayed for Hudson, pray too for Louisa. It's a matter of eternal life or eternal death for her, Amelia.'

Amelia shut the kitchen door and leaned against it. 'Lord God, I am sorry that I haven't loved her in the way I should have. God please bring Louisa to love you, help me to be as close to her as I am to Hudson. But Lord Jesus, please help me not to put either of them above you. I should love you most of all, more than anyone.'

Amelia quickly joined Hudson and Louisa in the parlour. Hudson had brought out his two pet squirrels and the two furry animals were causing havoc by climbing up the curtains.

'Help me Amelia,' laughed Hudson. 'Help me catch them before they destroy the place.'

***

After the family had enjoyed another meal, Mrs Taylor quickly cleaned up another pile of plates and cutlery. Hastily she shook the crumbs from off the linen table cloth out the back door. Soon, when all the dishes were washed and stacked away she eagerly took up her journal for a few more minutes scribbling. Lunch time had sparked off another memory which she wanted to share.

I remember when the children were quite young, I had been sitting at the dinner table comforting little Louisa who had just fallen off her chair. She had landed with quite a bump on the floor. This had given her quite a fright and she was a little bit upset.

The children had spent the day inside, rushing around and getting up to all sorts of mischief. I was flustered and fraught. I had not had a minute to myself all day and I was still physically exhausted after having nursed all the children through one sickness or another. Hudson had recovered from his last bout of fever but I was still very worried about him. It was hard to keep him cooped up inside but I could always bribe him with food - the promise of a nice piece of apple pie always worked wonders.

Anyway, Louisa was being comforted and Hudson as always was sitting at the dinner table waiting patiently. Everybody was munching away on their soup and bread. Well almost everybody. James had spent the day in the study going over the business accounts and some journals he subscribed to. He was now attempting to educate me about some new plan of his to send missionaries overseas to the Orient. Hudson sighed quietly as he sat at the table, waiting patiently.

Louisa was bolstered up now with more cushions so that she could reach her bowl of soup on the table but she still made a mess of the operation and slurped noisily.

'Louisa, if you don't learn to eat properly you shall have to eat your meals in the nursery and not with the big people.'

Louisa nodded obediently and then slurped again. I gave up - table etiquette would just have to wait for another day. Hudson sighed quietly, stared long and hard at his sister's bowl of soup and waited patiently.

Amongst all the hustle and bustle of a busy Taylor lunch-time I quickly glanced across at Hudson. 'He's not too happy today, is he?' I thought. But, before I could figure out what was bothering the little man, Amelia's petticoats and bloomers were on show right there in the middle of the dining room.

Amelia's head had done a quick flip and she was now staring underneath the linen cloth at the different pairs of feet peeping out from beneath the table. She was totally oblivious to the fact that her bloomers were on full show to the whole dining room. 'Amelia darling you are not behaving in a lady-like manner. Sit straight at the meal table, my dear. I don't want to send you back to the nursery with your sister.'

Amelia shuffled her bottom into a better position, nodded her head, and all of a sudden she burped. 'Beg your pardon, mother,' she muttered quickly before I could admonish her again. I just sat there. I tried to eat my soup but wasn't sure whether I should laugh or cry. Whichever of my female relatives had told me children should be seen and not heard had obviously never lived within a mile of the Taylor household. The little darlings sometimes drove me up the wall!

But once more Hudson sighed, stared at his sister's bowl of soup, stared at me and appeared to be waiting patiently - but for what? Poor Hudson, nobody was paying any attention to him. Everybody was munching away or slurping on their soup and no one was taking a blind bit of notice of the fact that he was the only person not eating anything... and he wasn't eating anything because he hadn't been given anything. All the lovely steaming bowls of vegetable soup had been served up but his flustered and fraught mother had missed him out. It must have happened when Louisa had slipped off her cushions. In the commotion of picking her up and 'kissing her better' Hudson's bowl of soup had been passed on to Amelia and nobody had said a word. But, because the children were not supposed to talk at the meal table unless an adult spoke to them first, Hudson didn't say a thing. He was a very serious little boy. Even though Amelia kept making eyes at him to say something there was no way he was going to. Our little man was just too polite for his own good. So he just sat there and sighed, waiting patiently. It was while I was wiping off some mushed up carrot from Louisa's chin that Hudson suddenly had an idea. There was a way he could speak up and draw attention to the fact that he had no soup... and it was quite within the rules. He was allowed to ask someone to pass the salt. His mother was sure to notice that he didn't have a bowl of soup to pour his salt into. If she didn't, then, any minute now, his stomach would growl so loudly he would definitely get a reaction.

'Could somebody please pass the salt?'

I turned round to look at Hudson's quivering little face. 'Of course Hudson, here you are. Oh Hudson! I'm sorry... your soup!' and with that I dashed out to the kitchen to bring in another bowl. Hudson's next sigh was one of contentment as he tucked into the delicious vegetable soup.

Right, now I have to get back to present day problems. We need to run through a final list with Hudson for his luggage. We have to make sure he has everything he needs before we start packing for the voyage. I'll likely not have any more time tonight to write in the journal.

***

After an early night Mrs Taylor slept soundly. She didn't even hear her husband clamber into bed with her as the clock struck ten. Neither did she hear the muffled conversation of the youngsters as they filed off to bed much later. But, as is quite often the case after an early night, she woke with the first cock crow, bright-eyed and quite rested. Now, what was she to do? It was far too early to make breakfast, but, if she wrapped up warmly, she could nip out for a quick walk. If she took her journal with her she might find a spot somewhere where she could scribble a few lines before coming back in to lay the table and get the fire going.

'I just have to have a little bit of freedom,' she said to herself. James Taylor was a dearly loved husband but sometimes, just sometimes, she wished he would let her off the leash a little bit. He was caring, devoted but quite domineering. She was, however, very proud of him. He was a chemist who actually did the work of a doctor. People had such faith in him. He could be generous to a fault and yet tight-fisted with his own flesh and blood. However Mrs Taylor adored him.

Hudson had had to leave school at an early age due to his poor health. He hadn't even been able to hold down a job for very long due to poor eyesight. Admittedly his health did improve and his family could easily have sent him to medical school but the decision was made by Mr Taylor to save the money and not to spend it on Hudson's education. Some of the family members didn't agree with Mr Taylor's decision but nobody openly questioned him.

Mrs Taylor understandably needed to be on her own sometimes. 'I just need time to myself,' she muttered into the cold morning air - and clouds of frosted breath rose up around her face. Like a child she puffed up her cheeks and blew with all her might. Mist rose up all around her as if she were a miniature steam train. Then she found a dry spot to sit on as she watched the sun rise over the near-by hill. As the earth thawed slightly so did her fingers and she began to gather more memories into her store.

'I think it's because I realise that Hudson only has a few more days to go before he leaves us. This little store of memories is something to remember him by. I know what, I'll write about what we got up to last night.'

We had such a 'do-you-remember session' last night. I even sang some songs for old time's sake and James called me 'his nightingale' once again. It's been so long since he called me that. I read out from this journal what I had written about 'The

31

soup episode' and Hudson laughed out loud! With tears in his eyes he turned to me and said 'I remember sitting there for ages desperately trying to work out how I was going to get Mother's attention.' His beautiful blue eyes sparkled as he laughed. 'Amelia was sitting there tucking into her soup. Louisa - well you had most of your soup on your chin or on the table cloth and there I was one very hungry little boy.' Then my young son said the most lovely thing, 'You know Mother, I will miss your soup!' James coughed awkwardly, so Hudson changed the subject. My James hates goodbyes.

Changing the mood completely, Hudson playfully reached his hand over behind Amelia and gave a quick tweak to her long sash. 'If you still wore plaits I would pull one for old times' sake!'

Amelia smiled back at him. Later, as I headed off to bed she asked me, 'Can't he see that I'm just about to burst into tears? I am going to miss him so much.' A quick hug and a kiss on her cheek and I told her she was being very brave.

Mrs Taylor remained gazing at the beautiful sunrise for a few more moments before continuing her walk. As she did so Amelia also got up and gazed out of her own bedroom window at the same sunrise. She'd been dreaming that night of Hudson, the Hudson she had known years ago. A little boy in breeches when she was a little girl in long plaits. Last night at the table he had reminded her about the way he used to pull them.

We used to have such adventures sometimes, out on our own, exploring places. I remember that afternoon when Hudson and I should have been helping Father in the store. Instead we ran off down towards Lunn Woods. There was a beautiful old church building in the distance where we would sometimes go exploring. The best thing, however, was that there were no adults in sight. We had freedom!

Like Mother, like daughter, young Amelia also liked to jot things down in her journal. It was a habit she had picked up from watching Mrs Taylor over the years. Amelia sat with her own leather-bound journal. These were memories to write down.

I remember charging after Hudson shouting, 'Hudson! I'll catch you I will.'

'No you won't' he yelled back. 'I'm faster than you!'

My little legs tried to keep up but Hudson was three years older, had skinny legs and a quick turn of speed.

'You're only faster because you are a silly-skinny,' I retorted.

'What did you say piggy-piggy oink-oink?' Hudson knew just what names to call me. I was so angry that I stopped mid-pace and squealed 'I'm not a pig! I'm just smaller.'

Hudson dashed up behind me pulled my plait and fled into the nearby wood. 'Smaller and rounder,' he said, giggling. He dashed behind an old oak tree and out of sight. I was really angry now! My little pink cheeks got pinker and I sped after my gangly-giggly brother. He always called me names and I would quite often lose my temper. All of a sudden I burst out laughing as he skidded on his bottom down a grassy slope, landing with his legs in the air. He looked stupid!

'Well, don't stand there. Give me a hand up, you silly sausage!' Stupidly I gave him my hand and he gave a big heave-ho and pulled me, bump, bump, down the slope too. I gave Hudson a quick smack round the ears and clambered back up the slope. 'Let's sit on top of the stile,' I suggested. We both raced to our own special spot on the old stone dyke.

'I love it here,' I whispered. The peace and quiet, the bird song, the beautiful flowers peeping out from the sweet meadow grass were sometimes just what I needed. Today there was no Louisa to tag along with me and no parents nagging about keeping my pinafore clean. Hudson sighed, 'I love it here too. Going on adventures is such fun!'

I giggled but Hudson suddenly felt a bit guilty.

'If Mother could see us she'd have a fit! We're not supposed to be here are we? But we won't be missed. We can stay out for ages yet.'

Just then my tummy rumbled really loudly. 'But Hudson I'm hungry,' I complained and with that he leapt off the stile and shouted, 'Piggy-piggy, oink-oink,' and made a dash for the edge of the field. Very soon he was clambering over the gate that led into the church yard.

'Oh bother that brother!' I grumbled.

Hudson looked back to see whether I was coming or not. But as always when I was sulking I was taking things slowly.

'Come on slow coach,' Hudson hollered.

Grumpy, tired and hungry, I kicked a stone against a grave. 'Look Hudson,' I said slightly surprised, 'does that grave say the numbers one and eight and three and two?'

Hudson looked at the grave. 'Yes it does. It says "In the year of our Lord Eighteen-hundred and thirty two." What does that mean?' he quizzed me.

Screwing up my face I pretended to work it out.

'Amelia! I'm always having to tell you stuff,' Hudson sighed. 'That means this person died in the year I was born. I was born in the year 1832. You were born three years after me of course, which means you are three years younger and that means I'm the boss!' With that Hudson pulled my plait again and dashed out through the gate. Rubbing the spot where he had yanked at my plait I yelled back at him, 'Says who?'

But he wasn't listening so I charged after him, pinafore and petticoat flapping in the breeze.

My little fat legs did their best to catch up but Hudson was already quite a bit down the lane and he was now doing some sort of mad leaping about. However, I was used to his strange ways by now. All Hudson could think of was how great it was to be outside after so long. He had spent three months cooped up in the house. Winter coughs and colds had kept him prisoner - sick in bed and feverish. Stretching his arms to the sky he laughed out loud, 'I'm free at last! Do what I like! Do what I please!'

Just then a roll of thunder sounded out from the dark clouds that were being chased by the cold Yorkshire wind. Silver grey rain-streaks spun out across the sky. Behind us rolled thick thunderheads, rumbling, with threatened rain and lightning. Very soon we were soaked through to our skins. I just picked up my skirts and ran - leaving Hudson to fend for himself. My little fat legs could go really fast when they wanted to.

Hudson stood there in the rain feeling really fed-up and already just a little bit sniffly. Little rivulets of rain water ran down his face and got in behind his shirt collar. He was wet, cold and miserable. As he turned the corner he was in sight of home and then another sight met him. 'Mother!' he gasped. He was in for it now!

The pony and trap were being led back behind the chemist's shop. Mother stood, waiting for him in the doorway. In a firm quiet voice she turned to him and said, 'Oh Hudson!'

Sheepishly he replied, 'Sorry Mother.'

I remember being sent up to my bedroom in disgrace. I was as tough as old boots. All I needed was a good rub down and a warm bed and I would be as bright as a button in the morning. Hudson, however, was always catching colds. He stood dripping in the hallway and suddenly he gave such a huge sneeze that it sent Mother into a frenzy. Quickly, she despatched her young son to the kitchen, where pans of water were put to boil and he was left to scrub down in the old tin bath.

'If you catch cold again you have only yourself to blame!' she admonished.

However, Hudson lay back in the warm bath water and did what he always did at times like these. He imagined his toes were big whales and his knees desert islands populated by China-men in bright flowing robes and long black pigtails. All of a sudden he piped up, 'Mother! Can I grow my hair in a pigtail mother? Please?'

'What nonsense will you think of next Hudson Taylor!' replied Mother. 'Pigtails? What a ridiculous idea!'

Beginning to leave

Mrs Taylor snuggled up in her coat to keep warm. A few more moments and then she would head off home. She had one last paragraph to write.

I remember how Hudson and Amelia loved to go on long country rambles. Often we would go down to Lunn Woods for what the children would call 'an adventure'. Sometimes Hudson and Amelia would take their hoops and race them down the lane, thoroughly enjoying themselves. Louisa would gather daisies and make long daisy-chains to tie round her hair. Hudson would sometimes take a little box or bag with him to collect things of interest on his travels. His room was filled with plants and stones and all sorts of collections. I didn't like the dead insects and butterflies so much, so Hudson hid these from me under his bed.

Meanwhile Amelia had nipped downstairs. When she had packed her journal away she had realised that she hadn't heard the usual noises from mother's room. Mother was almost always up before everybody, so where was she? A note on the kitchen table put Amelia's mind at ease. 'Out for a quick walk, love Mother.'

'Mother needs time to herself. Just like me,' Amelia said to herself. So she decided to make a start on the breakfast things and get the fire going. The back door creaked open. A rosy cheeked mother was blown in with a gust of wind and a sprinkling of dry leaves.

'Oh well done Amelia. I knew I could depend on you. Is the table laid? Yes! Excellent. Now do we have sugar and salt?' Mrs Taylor's gaze darted around the kitchen and the dining room - checking to see if there was anything she had missed.

Amelia looked inquisitively at her mother. 'What have you been up to?' she asked.

'Oh you know, Amelia, I just had to get out and spend some time on my own with God. I just sat on a dry stone dyke, writing my journal as the sun came up over the hedgerows.'

Amelia smiled, it had been just as she had pictured it. She noticed her mother's journal tucked into the pocket of her coat.

'I enjoyed what you read to us last night, Mother. It brought back a lot of memories. I should look out all my old journals. I really enjoyed writing down some memories of my own today.'

'Well done, Amelia. By the way, how are you and Louisa getting on?'

Amelia sighed. She had thought a lot about this. What Mrs Taylor had said to her about loving Louisa more, and praying for her, had really pricked her conscience. 'Mother, Louisa and I are getting on a lot better now. It's silly to squabble, but I do find it really annoying when she reads my journals without asking me. I know I've hurt her feelings in the past. I don't include her in what Hudson and I get up to and that's wrong, I know that. But Mother, I love her, really. Maybe she doesn't realise.'

Mrs Taylor smiled as she saw Louisa standing in the

doorway with a shocked look on her face. Louisa, still in her dressing gown, smiled warmly, 'It's all right Amelia, you don't have to tell me that. I know you love me. I love you too and I promise I won't read your journals ever again.' She paused and then added with a wink, 'Unless you let me.'

Amelia ruffled Louisa's hair. 'Oh, it doesn't really matter. You can read my journal any time you like. As long as you let me read yours!'

Giggling, Louisa's eyes twinkled, 'What a brilliant idea. That's exactly what we should do! Let's swap journals this afternoon for a laugh!'

Mrs Taylor was overjoyed. It was so good to see her two girls friendly once again. Quietly, she withdrew from the kitchen, leaving them to their plans. Besides, she had a house to run, and a sleepy husband to wake up.

***

The chat at the breakfast table was centred around China, once again. Hudson was anxiously explaining to Louisa what it meant for him to know that he was finally going to the country God had called him to. As Amelia cleared the breakfast dishes she lifted up a royal blue milk jug from off its spot on the linen table cloth.

'Look at that stain Hudson! Do you remember making that?'

Hudson laughed. 'Yes, I do. You were asking me, Louisa, about the first time I realised I had to go to China! Well, that's when that stain happened. I made it. I always was a bit of a clumsy idiot, wasn't I, Amelia?'

Amelia teased Hudson openly about his two left feet.

Mrs Taylor gazed at the stain. No matter how much she had scrubbed, it hadn't shifted. She must have written that episode in her journal somewhere. 'I should go and look it out,' she thought to herself.

***

Later that evening she came across the old journal. The writing was faded. 'But it's still legible,' Mrs Taylor muttered, as she skimmed through the journal.

Meal times in our house are never dull. Today, as usual, we were discussing China and all things oriental.

'But, my dear, this article on China is so amazing!' said my excited husband - the local expert on the Far East and the Orient. 'This article has certainly re-kindled my interest in this part of the globe I can assure you.' As far as I was concerned this interest of his had never needed any 're-kindling'. China is an ever constant topic of conversation with friends and guests at our dinner table. But still, I am pleased that he has interests outside the chemist's and the demands of our young family. It keeps his mind active, stretches his imagination and keeps him content. And I do find these stories that he tells very interesting and lively. It is certainly good to remember these countries in prayer. Our family always prays for China. So, in a way, the fiasco at dinner was no surprise. But I digress. In the midst of our conversation I noticed that James' tea cup was empty.

'Do continue dear. Would you like more beef tea?'

'Well, yes, just a spot. Thank you.' Mr Taylor then continued. 'You see the Chinese have better education than the West. Did you know that they can all read?'

'Really?' I said, intrigued.

'Yes, they have such respect for the printed word that no-one would destroy even a page of any publication. Now children let's have a test of your knowledge. Who can answer these questions? What empire is over one hundred times the size of

39

England and occupies one-tenth of the area of the earth's surface where people can live?'

Hudson shouted out, 'China!'

'Yes! Excellent. Now, if all the Chinese were ordered to stand in single file, with a yard between each of them, how many times would they circle the globe at its equator?'

'Seven times,' shouted Amelia, just in front of Hudson.

'Well done, Amelia. Next question. Name four things the Chinese have invented.'

Hudson thought hard. 'Gun powder, the compass, paper and the art of printing.'

'Top marks, Hudson. The quiz is finished, now let me have my tea.' Turning to me he added, 'It's such a pity, though, that so few Chinese know about salvation. There is such an opportunity there, my dear. The Christian church should simply flood China with missionaries. We should send shiploads of Bibles to these poor people. Imagine not having ever read a Bible in your life. Imagine not even being able to see or hold one. China is in desperate need of the good news of Jesus Christ! We must flood China with missionaries. We must flood China with the word of God.'

He hurriedly sipped some more of his beef tea but had no idea of the effect this conversation was having on the silent young lad by his side. Hudson was enthralled. The very word China thrills him and sends shivers down his spine. At twelve years old the tales of eastern-promise make his heart beat fast and his eyes twinkle. He daydreams of sailing to undiscovered countries. But this time it was different. His father shouted loudly, 'This is what we should do! Flood China with Bibles.' His fist hit the table and the tea pot wobbled. 'We should tell these people about Jesus! That country is lost.' James added almost in a whisper, 'But who would go to such a far away land?'

Crash-bang-wallop! Hudson leapt up from his seat with a hearty, 'I'll go! I'll do it!' Amelia gawked at her big brother, Louisa giggled. We all looked at where Louisa was pointing and saw that Hudson's beef tea had spilt all over the white linen table cloth.

'Hudson!' I cried. 'I'll never get that stain out!'

Flushed I rushed to get a cloth. James looked at the fervent, enthusiastic face of his son. He smiled. The very idea of sickly little Hudson sailing to China was almost laughable. However, we did exchange brief glances. Just for a second we both remembered that day we had dedicated our son to the Lord. Often when Hudson speaks animatedly of China we do wonder. Does God have plans to send him there?

But James turned and looked Hudson in the eye. 'China's not for you son. Sit down while your mother cleans the table.'

Hudson blushed a deep red. It's a shame. His heart is in the right place. God is definitely working in his life, but as his father said, China is not for him. It can't be. Can it?

Mrs Taylor packed the old journal away once again.

'Now Hudson is one week away from sailing to China! Who would believe it! Sickly little Hudson! God is amazing. Who can understand his ways?'

Beginning to believe

Sitting together on the rug in front of the fire Amelia and Louisa poured over their old journals. 'Where is mother?' asked Louisa.

'She is through in the kitchen. She will join us shortly,' Amelia replied.

Amelia leafed through a few of her old notebooks until she found what she was looking for. A faded childlike hand had written in the corner of an old exercise book, 'I love Jesus. My name is Amelia Taylor. I came to love Jesus today. I want Hudson to love Jesus.' Further entries throughout the journals were in the same vein. Louisa popped her head over her sister's shoulder to have a look at what she was reading. 'Did you write that?' she asked. 'Yes. I did. This journal is full of little notes like that. "Prayed for Hudson today." "If only Hudson would come to Jesus and ask for forgiveness." I wrote that one after Father caught Hudson blaspheming.'

'Never!' Louisa gasped. 'Hudson was cursing God! Hudson?' Amelia blushed. 'Yes Louisa! He's changed now, thank God. But it was very difficult for a time. Perhaps you don't remember? I do, however.' Mrs Taylor wandered in and sat with the girls. 'Hudson is through helping your father with the prescriptions. Is this another trip down memory lane?'

Amelia turned and looked at her mother. Both of them had found that time very hard. She picked up her journal and read out loud.

Hudson has just been so restless today. I don't understand him. He just gets so frustrated and angry and then stalks off for long walks in the country. He used to take me with him on his long walks, now he wants nothing to do with any of us. In fact he wants nothing to do with God. That is what hurts me the most.

Father God you know that when I first came to you all I wanted was for Hudson to be the same. I have such a peace in my heart, your love has given me that. Even when I am hurt, afraid and everything in my life seems so dark, I can turn to you and you are a light. You comfort me. Hudson seems to be wandering around in his own world of darkness and it looks as though he intends to stay there. I can have questions, and problems, but when I turn to you in prayer or read what you want to tell me in the Bible, these questions are answered. Sometimes you don't answer my questions the way I expect, but you give me such a peace in my heart anyway, I feel I can go on, as I know that you are in control.

Hudson's job in the local bank isn't helping him at all. Why did he ever go and get a job there? It has just changed him completely. The type of young man who works there is not the type of young man I would want Hudson to be. And I see him becoming more and more like them every day. All they care about it what fun they can have when they are finished at work. All they want is to make lots of money so that they can have all this fun. They want to drink themselves stupid, lark around and just behave like silly sops. Hudson now wants to live in a fine house, so he says, with horses to go hunting with. I don't know where he will get that sort of money. He wastes most of his money anyway. He is so popular at work. He is merry and bright with his friends. I see them in the street. But as soon as he comes in the door of his own house, as soon as he is in the company of his own family he is sullen, bad mannered and moody. He is a right misery!

Lord Jesus, I am sorry, but there are times when I would rather not spend time with him. But I know I must take every opportunity to bring him to you! It is just so frustrating! Whenever I try to speak about you to Hudson, he turns on me and laughs. Lord, I don't want to bring your name up in conversation, only to have your name treated as a joke. Thankfully he is not totally depraved, as yesterday he apologised to me when I burst into tears. He had been cursing and swearing again. I just couldn't stand it and fled out of the parlour to my bedroom. Poor little Louisa didn't know what was going on! But to be honest he hasn't really changed and if he were really sorry he would stop doing what upsets me and mother so much.

I know his behaviour upsets you too, Lord Jesus. That is the worst part of all. He carries on treating your name like dirt. All the apologies in the world mean nothing unless he feels so sorry that he actually says sorry from his heart to you and asks you to help him! I wish I could do something God! Perhaps he doesn't take any notice of me because I am young. He is three years older than me and thinks of me as his silly, little, sister.

Amelia stopped reading. Louisa looked shocked. She didn't remember much of this at all. 'I remember you and Hudson disagreeing once or twice and I think I remember him being a bit sulky. I didn't realise it was as bad as this. What a change there has been in him then!'

'Yes!' Mrs Taylor agreed. 'He left the bank in 1848 and came to work for Father at the chemist's doing small prescriptions. Nothing exciting. His eye infection meant he couldn't hold down a job at the bank. His eyes couldn't cope with the strain. This meant he was still frustrated, bored and unsettled. All of a sudden he was becoming a young man and he couldn't cope with it.

'Perhaps we didn't allow him enough freedom. Maybe he was cooped up too much. Working at home and living at home was very hard and he wanted his independence. But the very thing that both Amelia and I knew would soothe his soul and give him the peace he was searching for, was the thing he avoided most in all the world. He had absolutely no time for God. His soul was missing a Saviour. Yet the Lord, Jesus Christ, did not feature in Hudson Taylor's plans.'

Mrs Taylor sighed. Amelia held her mother's hand and then continued.

'Despite our disagreements and the division between us, it was to me that Hudson would turn, when things got too much. The tension between him and Father was so thick you could have cut it with a knife. Father couldn't understand what Hudson was going through and the change in his personality and life style. Hudson found Father more and more frustrating. I think he found his prayers long and tiresome, he couldn't understand Father at all. They both began to irritate each other more and more. Hudson saw Father as pompous and infuriating. Father saw Hudson as disobedient and ungrateful.

'I then decided I had to do something. The only thing I could do was pray. So I promised God and myself that I would pray for Hudson every day until the day that he gave himself totally to God. To remind myself of this promise I wrote it down, here, in this journal.'

Louisa bent over to look at the journal. Amelia picked up another and continued the story. 'Then one day when Mother was away on holiday, I went out for a walk leaving Hudson at home. It was then that something happened. Several days later I wrote it down in my journal. It was the month of June and the year was 1849.'

I can hardly believe it! It's just too amazing! I feel as if I have finally managed to get wings for one day! Hudson has given himself to Christ. He has turned to Jesus. He has asked him to come into his heart. Hudson now belongs to God! My prayers have been answered. Praise God!

It happened on the half holiday. Mother doesn't know yet. She doesn't come back for another three days and Hudson has instructed me not to say anything! But oh, I feel as if I am about to burst and if I don't write it down in my journal I shall burst! That afternoon I had gone out for a walk and Hudson was bored as usual. With Father out of the study, on some errand or other, Hudson leafed through some of the pamphlets Father keeps there in a basket. In the basket was a collection of popular Gospel tracts. They weren't very popular with Hudson but he picked one out because he was so bored he had to do something. He had a brief look at the tract and then thought that it was short enough not to be too difficult and that he could probably read the story and put it to the side before it got too preachy. Hudson just couldn't stand getting preached at. It's funny writing that in the past tense! But anyway, as far as Hudson was concerned he would read the story and forget about the moral.

Hudson nipped out to the old warehouse to read in peace. He snuggled down planning to read the story and then snooze. However, as he read, one sentence gripped him. Suddenly he realised that he had been approaching religion from the wrong angle altogether. Christianity was not meant to be a dreary struggle - trying to pay for all the times you had been bad by being good. Hudson had long given up trying to be a Christian because he had felt it was just far too difficult. He thought, 'I can never manage it. Being good is too difficult. God's standards are just too high. I may as well give up!'

But as he read he discovered that in actual fact he didn't have to pay God anything - it had already been paid. Jesus had paid the penalty for Hudson. There was nothing more to do. Salvation was free. Christianity did not mean struggling away, year after year, in the hope of being good enough to get to heaven. 'Jesus Christ simply asked me to fall down on my knees and accept him as my saviour, to accept his free gift of salvation and to praise his name for ever!' Hudson has been enthusing about it ever since! 'It was like a light had flashed straight into my soul' he keeps saying time and time again! And I love to hear him!

Louisa looked at Amelia. Amelia's eyes twinkled. A smile spread all over her face. Excitedly she turned to her mother. 'But what about you! You've got another part of the story to tell. Did you write anything down about that?'

Mrs Taylor thought for a moment, then dashed upstairs to get another journal.

'What has she gone to get?' quizzed Louisa.

'Well, remember I said that mother didn't know about Hudson,' laughed Amelia. Louisa nodded.

'As it happened I wasn't quite right about that. All I knew was that mother was away from home and I was the only one Hudson had told so far. However,' Amelia paused as her mother settled herself down on the couch again, 'I hadn't reckoned for the amazing power of God! Come on Mother, read out what you wrote that day!'

Slightly breathless Mrs Taylor began to flick through an old journal. 'What I first wrote was just a small quick paragraph. It all happened on the afternoon of the half day holiday - the same time that Hudson was in the barn preparing for a quick read and a snooze.'

Something happened today. I know my prayers have been answered. I have prayed all afternoon for Hudson. I locked myself away in my room while my sister and her family were out visiting. I had found myself with several hours to spare and knew that I had to spend them in prayer for my young son. I also had this deep conviction to pray and pray until my prayers were answered.

I prayed that he would finally change, that God would at last take over my young son's life. He is seventeen years of age and is wasting his life. But now I am so sure that my prayers have been answered, even though I am eighty miles away, I can now change that to the past tense. He is seventeen years of age and was wasting his life, until Hudson Taylor came, this afternoon, to know and love his saviour, the Lord Jesus Christ. After hours of heartfelt prayer I have a peace straight from God!

'You knew?' exclaimed Louisa.

'Yes, Louisa, I knew. God came to me in another town, eighty miles away and told me to pray for your brother. I had such a feeling, in fact it almost wasn't a feeling but more like a voice, but not the kind of voice you hear with your ears - more the kind you hear in your heart. I knew that I must pray for Hudson. There was something happening that needed the power of prayer. There is no other way to describe it. God wanted me to get into prayer completely, to pray with all my strength. I've heard Hudson describe it as 'doing a business transaction with God'. That afternoon it was as though God was inviting me into his office, into his presence to present my case, to tell my Creator how I longed for my son's salvation. Even now I don't totally understand it. God is so amazing. So deep. Yet he comes to us and actually wants to be with us. We don't deserve his love. God is so wonderful.'

Mrs Taylor became lost in thought as she turned to gaze out the window. 'Hudson told all his friends at the bank about his new love for God. The sparkle was back in his eyes. Our prayers had been answered. In fact it was during that summer that Hudson and Amelia stopped coming to church in the evening.'

Louisa looked puzzled and then smiled. 'Oh yes I remember. They handed out tracts instead. I thought you were brave but I was embarrassed for you too.'

Mrs Taylor smiled, 'There is no need to be ashamed of Christ, Louisa. Once you realise what Christ has done for you, you are compelled to tell others about your amazing saviour.' Louisa blushed slightly and was quiet. Amelia thought silently, 'Louisa still doesn't love Jesus.'

Mrs Taylor continued with her tale, 'Well the time came for Amelia to go to school. She was becoming a young lady, so we sent her to your aunt's school in Barton-upon-Humber. That winter wasn't so easy as there was still friction between Father and Hudson. Then in December of the following year Hudson anxiously prayed to God about his sin. He was convicted about something which was bothering him a lot. He promised God that he would do anything if only God would keep him from the awful sins that frightened him so much. He then had the same experience I had - a voice spoke into the centre of his soul as loudly as though it had been spoken right into his ear! "Then go to China!" it said.

'From that hour his mind was made up! Even as a child he had been interested in China and had wanted to tell the Chinese about God. Now he realised that he had to do something about it!'

Smoothing her skirt as she got up off the couch she added, 'A lot of water has gone under the bridge since 1849. Now it's September 1853 and your brother leaves in a week or so for China. I'm still not used to the idea.'

Amelia and Louisa both got up off the rug in unison and ran to hug their mother. Thankfully, she still had her two girls. Mrs Taylor hugged them back. God had been very good to her she realised.

***

That evening, when the family Bible was back on the shelf Amelia and Louisa went to bed. Louisa quickly fell asleep. Gentle breathing sounded from beneath the quilt and Amelia smiled. Now she would have some peace and quiet. There were still some old journal entries and letters she wanted to read. 'Hmm, here's a letter from Hudson in 1850.

> Poor neglected China! Scarcely anyone cares about it... that immense country, which contains nearly a fourth of the human race, is left in ignorance and darkness.

'Now what sparked that letter I wonder?'

Amelia thought back to the year of 1850 and remembered all the disappointment Hudson had suffered when no one could catch his vision for China. 'I suppose they took one look at him, eighteen years of age, no university education, skinny and sickly and barely able to stand up to the damp and chill of Yorkshire. People just laughed at the very idea of Hudson going to China. Who could blame them?'

Placing the letter down on the quilt she rummaged in the box until she found the journal that corresponded with the year 1850. When she had been away at school, Amelia had received frequent letters from Hudson, telling her all that he was up to. She flicked through the pages until she came to a bit she recognised.

Poor Hudson! I feel sorry for myself away at school, but he is putting himself through the wringer and no mistake, and all with the aim of toughening himself up! The general impression that some people have of Hudson is that he is too soft, too weak and definitely not the type that should travel half way across the world to China! So he is setting himself out a strict and stringent regime to tackle this problem! Father has had to take his feather bed out of his room. I think he is either sleeping on boards or some blankets! In addition to this he has started to go on long walks on the moors. He says the fresh air is good for him and that the cold air toughens him up. And as if that wasn't enough, on top of learning one of the most difficult languages in the world, he has decided to improve his general education! Hudson's heart is full of China!

However, his heart is also full of something else, or should I say someone else. Is it possible to have your heart full of two things? I don't know. But anyway, his heart is also full of Miss Vaughan, and that's lovely, because she is my music teacher and she is a darling. She is beautiful, accomplished and with a wealthy father. Ever since I took Miss Vaughan home with me for the holidays Hudson's letters have been full of China and Miss Vaughan, Miss Vaughan and China. He is besotted with Miss Vaughan and totally committed to China. He is stricken with Miss Vaughan's 'varied accomplishments', her 'genteel nature' and of course her 'striking good looks'. On November 11th he wrote, and I quote,

'What can I do? I know I love her. To go without her would make the world a blank. But I cannot bring her to want.'

It's the same old story. Our family is not of the same social standing as Miss Vaughan's and if Hudson goes to China he will be even poorer. Hudson being poor is a horrible thought and sends shivers down my spine. However, God will provide. I worry about him being cold and hungry in deepest, darkest China. I worry that Miss Vaughan is only toying with him and that she will break his heart.

Amelia sighed, Miss Vaughan brought back

memories. When Hudson had been employed by a doctor, in Hull, in the spring of 1851, Miss Vaughan and Amelia had seen a lot of him. Barton, where Amelia went to school, was just a ferry ride across the Humber, the large grey river that cut through the busy town of Hull. Hudson was a frequent passenger on that ferry. He enjoyed those times.

Amelia giggled as she remembered the dewy eyed brother who gazed adoringly at the 'beautiful' Miss Vaughan, 'exquisitely' playing the piano. He would sigh as he discussed the 'grace and poise' with which she sang, the 'intelligent wit' she used in conversations and the 'sumptuous but discreet' taste she had in all her attire. If Amelia hadn't loved Miss Vaughan as a friend and teacher, she would have been sick of the sound of her name.

Then there was that holiday the three of them had taken to the Peak District. It had been such fun, horse riding from dawn to dusk, out in the fresh, bracing, peak air. That holiday had clinched it and from then on Hudson Taylor was madly in love with Miss Marianne Vaughan. However, Marianne was only politely interested in China and Hudson just kept raising his hopes. Amelia sighed and read her journal again. 'Oh! I remember this bit.'

What am I going to tell Hudson! Miss Vaughan says China is not for her! Do I tell him? Does he know?

Then later on.

It's strange to write this, but I actually believe that Hudson realises the situation with Miss Vaughan. He just does not want to admit it. He loves her, I'm sure. His heart is never flippant. He knows that China is going to be a life of poverty and hardship, so cannot bring himself to ask Miss Vaughan to give up wealth and security at home, for poverty and danger in China. But even as I write this I hear that Hudson is coming over to Barton to visit us. He has specifically mentioned Miss Vaughan in his note! I am very unsure about this!

Amelia sighed and tucked all the letters and journals back in the box. She was tired and her eyes were struggling to stay awake. One puff and the candle was out, but her mind didn't sleep as quickly as Louisa's had. 'I think this Miss Vaughan fiasco is over but has Hudson laid it to rest? His heart is so vulnerable. The engagement is definitely off. Her father was the cause of that. I remember the letter Hudson showed me.

Were you to remain in England nothing would give me more pleasure than to see you happily united to Marianne. But I can never think of her leaving the country.

Amelia closed her eyes, 'Lord, send Hudson someone to love him and look after him.' With that prayer she slept.

The Journey Begins

Next morning Mr Taylor took the Bible down from the sideboard and the family worshipped God together. Today, from their family, someone was leaving to obey Christ's command to 'Go into all the world and preach the gospel'. Amelia's heart sang as she thought on these words, though her eyes wept. Many times in the past she had prayed for Hudson. Many times she had cried over him. However, God had a plan for Hudson and as always God's plan was done in God's time.

Worship over, the fire in the parlour crackled as Amelia curled herself up in an armchair. She smiled at Hudson who was now, anxiously, waiting for his coach to arrive. It would not be long before he left to fulfil a major part of God's plan for him. Louisa had began to sniffle a bit.

'Come on now girls!' Hudson urged. 'No floods of tears, not now, not today. I don't like to see either of my sisters crying. Here I have a present for both of you. It's just something to remember me by when I am gone.' Louisa let out a loud sob as Hudson brought out his pair of pet squirrels from behind the cabinet.

'They're your squirrels Hudson!' Louisa was blubbering now. Amelia didn't know whether to laugh or cry as the squirrels squirmed and wriggled in Hudson's hands. 'Look after them now,' he said, trying to return them to their cage. 'They will miss me I am sure.' Louisa promised faithfully to look after them always. Amelia looked towards the window. Father was helping lift some crates and a valise out on to the road. Mother was anxiously overseeing everything as efficiently as ever. Amelia said quietly, 'We will, all three of us, be brave today. It doesn't matter how far apart we are. We're together for ever! Aren't we?' and with that Amelia heard in the distance the sound of carriage wheels and the snap of a rider's whip.

'That will be my ride,' Hudson said and hurriedly left the room. China beckoned. Amelia stood and held Louisa's hand as their excitable, enthusiastic, entertaining brother exited the room. He was leaving them now.

***

'Is that the last item, Mrs Taylor?' the coachman asked politely as Mrs Taylor anxiously surveyed all the luggage piled on top. There wasn't that much. Hudson's other possessions had been sent on previously.

The coach was just a small local service which would drop Hudson off at the main coach for Tottenham. Mrs Taylor would accompany Hudson on the first leg of his journey. She and her husband would then meet him at Liverpool in a few day's time. The missionary society had arranged for Hudson to do two meetings before he set sail. He would then rejoin his parents in Liverpool before boarding on the sailing vessel *The Dumfries* bound for Shanghai.

'I think we are all accounted for.' Hudson extracted

himself from the iron like grip of his sisters to help his mother into the carriage. The horses were whinnying and stamping their feet - anxious to get going. Hudson turned to give both girls another bear hug. 'I'll miss you both! I don't know what else to say.' With that he leapt into the carriage, shut the door and told the driver to be on his way. The whip cracked and the horses strode off down the high street. Amelia frantically ran after the disappearing coach, waving her handkerchief and calling out, 'Goodbye! Goodbye! Remember to write!'

***

The coach ride had been fairly uneventful. Hudson had written several letters that he had given his mother to post. She stood holding them as Hudson climbed up into his next coach. Hudson wrote letters to Amelia and Louisa. Mrs Taylor noticed that there were no letters to Marianne Vaughan. She was glad. Perhaps Hudson was over that broken romance. However there was a letter to a Miss Sissons.

'Why is he writing her?' she wondered. 'It's none of my business I suppose. He can write to whoever he wants without my permission.' But alarm bells rang in her head. She knew her son too well. He fell in love easily. These last few weeks before he left for China made him especially vulnerable. Hudson desperately wanted to get married. But China was more important.

'Few women will leave home comforts for a life of uncertainty and poverty. Hudson will have to learn to live a single life - perhaps for the rest of his life. Lord God,' Mrs Taylor prayed, 'comfort him, look after him.'

Mrs Taylor was glad this was not the final farewell. In a few days time she would see Hudson once again in Liverpool - she would say goodbye then. Smoothing down her dress before she got back into the coach she tried to think about other things. There were arrangements to make on her return home. She thought about the small problems of cases and packing and not about the big problems of a young son and his mammoth journey.

The following morning an extremely tired and worn out mother struggled out of bed to plan her day and the remainder of their travel arrangements to Liverpool. Absent-mindedly she brushed her silver grey hair. Vacantly staring in the mirror, her thoughts wandered.

Years had rolled by since the birth of her little son. 1832 had seen James Hudson Taylor come screeching into the world. Uniting the names of the two families, Hudson and Taylor, he united their hopes that the Lord would indeed do amazing things through the life of this little baby.

But Lord there were times that I doubted. I doubted that he would live some nights. I worried that he would never give his life to you. It was difficult. Then there was that night when he exclaimed that he wanted to go to China! Cups flying, tea everywhere! What a shock it was to think back to what I had said twelve years past. 'I am ready now to give myself, my child and my children to you.' Then, the very thought of Hudson going to China was so ridiculous Lord, I could have laughed were it not for this quiet whisper in my heart... "set apart unto the Lord."

Rising from the dressing table she splashed cold water on her face. She rummaged in the drawer of her bedside cabinet and pulled out her spectacles. Sitting on the edge of the bed, with a dozing husband still beneath the sheets, she murmured, 'I will just re-read some of these verses in Exodus and Numbers for old times' sake. Lord, he is yours and not mine any more.'

As she leafed through the old familiar Bible verses, the firm, gentle arm of her husband reached round and hugged his anxious wife. Husband and wife, between them, re-dedicated their son to the Lord.

***

The docklands at Liverpool were a hive of activity. Hudson and his parents were now re-united and Hudson's London meeting had gone well. He was ready to set sail for the Orient. His mother was not so ready to let him. Though Amelia and Louisa remained at home other friends and family were in Liverpool to see the young Hudson away on his voyage. They all met up at the Owen Hotel to say their farewells.

The whole of Liverpool seemed to lurch and heave with traders and dockland traffic. Coaches and carriages everywhere were taking this or that merchant from the docklands to the city centre. Carts, stacked high with wares and goods to send to the Orient, fought each other for space in the area surrounding the gangway. *The Dumfries* was getting ready to sail. Mr Taylor checked with the port authorities to find out when the final boarding was. However he discovered that there was a problem.

'Oh now... let's see Sir, I think there has been a delay with that vessel. Yes. I'm sorry, urgent but minor repairs you understand. The ship is in fine form - there is no need to worry- but it is far better for all concerned if the repairs are dealt with now. You can't risk sending a ship half -way across the world. At best she'd arrive limping into Shanghai. Wouldn't look good would it?' Mr Taylor sighed, he must go back to Barnsley alone. He could not leave the chemist's for any longer and Amelia and Louisa were at home alone. 'It's best if I go home.' Mr Taylor hastened to pack his belongings.

'But Hudson would love you to be here when he leaves,' Mrs Taylor pleaded.

'I know that, but I can't wait until the 19th, it's just too long. You understand Hudson?' Mr Taylor anxiously looked towards his son.

'Yes Father, I do. God bless and give the girls my love.'

A berth was soon arranged for Mr Taylor on the train back to Yorkshire. Hudson stood beside his mother and father as they huddled together on the station platform. It would not be long now before Mr Taylor's train arrived. A few moments later, in a flurry of steam and smoke, the train pulled into the station and Mr Taylor hugged his son, kissed his wife and leapt on board. There was a tear in his eye, which nobody mentioned, and then the whistle blew. A belch of smoke and steam covered the platform as the train began to pull out of the station. Hudson ran along the platform waving to his father through the carriage window. Hudson's eyes met his father's and he saw there what he had always known had existed, his father's love. He remembered the mornings he had spent as a child praying with his father. Hudson, Amelia, William (when he had been alive) and young Louisa had come into their father's room, each day, where he had knelt in prayer beside them, his strong arms surrounding them. The love of their father on earth drew a picture for them of the far better love of their Heavenly Father.

Now that the train had gone and Mr Taylor was out of sight, Hudson and his Mother spent the next few days exploring Liverpool and daily checking with the port authorities about the sea worthiness of *The Dumfries*. The 19th of September finally arrived and Hudson and his Mother found themselves walking up the gangway to inspect what would be Hudson's quarters for the next six months or so. Two friends accompanied Mrs Taylor onboard to say goodbye to Hudson. Mrs Taylor hoped they would have some time alone before she had to leave.

'This is it,' she sighed to herself as Hudson heaved one of his bags to a waiting sailor. Mrs Taylor, mother, friend, guardian and protector was now fulfilling the final duty in the role she had assumed twenty-one years ago.

Hudson offered his hand to help his mother on board *The Dumfries*. She breathed in the sharp, salty, Mersey air. The cool wind came in off the ocean ushering away the stale smell of fish, oil, grease and city life. It was a relief to have fresh air in her lungs, to be away from the busy, bustling Liverpool.

Inside the cabin she looked about her. She would picture him here, reading, writing and dreaming when she did the same, by their log fire in Yorkshire. Perhaps this picture was rather optimistic as Hudson would probably spend the first week with his head in a bucket, struggling against sea sickness. Hudson tried the small bunk for size. 'Oh well, it's a bit on the short side, but I shall sleep curled up, so I shan't notice it too much.' There is a chest here which I will use for my bits and pieces. My Bible and books can fit in too.'

Together, mother and son, unpacked clothes and laid them neatly in a small closet, built into the side of the wall. None of the furniture was loose or free standing. At the first big wave anything that was not attached to the floor, or to the walls, would be sent flying and could in fact injure someone. Hudson's small bunk bed was nailed heavily to the side wall and two drawers slid out from underneath. Both drawers had a strong catch on them, to stop them falling open and spilling any contents on the floor. The closet was at the foot of the bed and a small chest cabinet was at its side.

The noise and racket increased steadily as more and more cargo was brought on board. Coming on board early had been a good idea. Hudson was settled in, in good time, and now the two of them could sit and enjoy each other's company while watching the busy world of the merchant sea men frantically pass them by. The two friends left the mother and son to say their last goodbyes alone. Mrs Taylor was thankful for that.

A large load of merchant goods swung high above them and was then lowered, on a rope, into the hold below. Men ran up and down the gangway with bundles, hunching their shoulders and backs. The noise of hard work and creaking boards mingled with shouted orders from the overseers. There was no noise from anxious relatives and friends as Hudson was the only passenger on board this vessel. A loud call was heard from the other side of the ship, 'All ashore that's going ashore.'

'Oh Hudson! So soon?' gasped Mrs Taylor.

'Don't worry,' Hudson assured her, 'We have time to pray. They won't raise the gangway yet.'

Together they sat on Hudson's bunk bed. Mrs Taylor smoothed the covers while picturing Hudson's own snug bed at home. This bed wasn't so comfortable looking but it would be warm and hopefully dry.

Their spirits lifted as they sang a hymn together. Old sailors rushing past the cabin, stopped for a moment to listen to "The Nightingale" sing. Hudson saw some smile softly. Perhaps these rough men had in their murky pasts mothers who had sung hymns to them. Hudson then prayed to God for protection for his mother on her return journey and for his whole family as he left them to follow God's calling, to China.

'Lord Jesus, look after every single person that I love and hold dear. Lord you know how lonely I will be without them.' He faltered slightly. The anxious eyes of his mother looked at the strained face of her son. She felt his pain. This was no longer the thing they had planned for, it was no longer the day they had looked forward to. This was the journey to China, this was the day he would leave them. The point of no return. As Hudson's words stumbled and faltered she did something simple but so beautiful. Bending over she kissed his cheek.

'Everything will be fine my child. We won't forget you. You will be in our prayers. Never forget why it is that you are leaving me. If it wasn't for the fact that you were leaving to follow God, no ship on this earth could take you from me. But because you are going to serve our Lord, there is nothing on this earth that will persuade me to keep you.'

Hugging him close she looked into the deep lilac eyes, mirror images of her own.

'May the Lord bless thee and keep thee. May the Lord make his face shine upon thee and be gracious unto thee. May the Lord lift up his countenance upon thee and give thee peace.'

Just then the two friends entered the cabin, once again, to pray with Hudson before the ship set sail. All prayed in turn and Hudson read a psalm before Mrs Taylor turned to smooth her son's bed for the last time. With that she lifted her skirt and Hudson escorted her on to the deck - only to discover that the ship had actually been cast off and was beginning to edge away from the wharf. Quickly Hudson and the deck hands managed to get Mrs Taylor, and the others, safely on shore. 'Give my love to Amelia and Louisa and wish Amelia a happy birthday from me,' urged Hudson. Mrs Taylor turned pale as she saw his face disappearing. She collapsed in a heap on the dockside and began to shake all over. Hudson took a huge risk and leapt ashore and put his arm around her.

'Dear Mother, don't cry. We shall meet again. Think about why I am leaving you, as you said, "It's not for wealth or fame, but to try and bring the Chinese to the knowledge of Jesus."'

As the ship drifted further from her moorings, Hudson managed to jump aboard again and run to his cabin. The final groanings of *The Dumfries*'s anchor sounded out across the dockside as it was hoisted up, creaking and protesting, from the soft Mersey mud. *The Dumfries* set off towards the dock gates. All the time a small anxious figure, huddled below on the quayside, searched the side of the ship for one last glimpse of her son. But she could not see him. Her heart sank. Where was he? Was he all right? Had his feelings got the better of him? She hated to picture him huddled behind the rigging, weeping.

'Hudson! Hudson! Are you all right? Where are you? God where is he? Let me see him again, just once, please.'

Just then the tall gangly figure appeared again, at the stern of the boat. He was waving frantically, something clenched in his hand. He brought his arm back behind his shoulder,

'Why, he is going to throw something to me!' she gasped. Hudson hurled something small and black over the near side of the boat and onto the ground by her feet. She frantically grasped beneath her skirt for the object. It was his pocket Bible. On the front page he had scrawled, 'The love of God which passeth knowledge - JHT.' Just then the ship hit the deeper waters of the Mersey as they passed the dock gates. The Mersey was now this huge gulf between mother and child. Hudson climbed up into the rigging to get a better view of his mother but he heard her before he saw her, weeping at the end of the pier.

This was no fool's errand he was on. Hudson had counted the cost. He knew it was going to be difficult.

'Lord God, I am not leaving my family out of some self-centred desire. If you hadn't called me, I would not be leaving my mother crying there. Yet your tears are full of more anguish than hers. Your heart is full of more love than ours. It is an honour to suffer for you.' Hudson's voice caught on a sob as sailors and deck hands rushed about him. No one paid any attention to the weeping of yet another passenger, headed off to goodness knows where. They were too interested in rigging masts and coastal currents. Hudson wiped away the tears to catch a last glimpse of his mother - who was now just a small dark figure huddled amongst friends and relatives on the Mersey dockside.

Clutching the Bible, Mrs Taylor stared out to sea. Her breath came in short gasps, hot tears stung her eyes. Friends and relatives surrounded her as she struggled to support herself. Leaving her to gather her fraught emotions together, the well wishers retreated a pace or too.

'She needs some privacy - leave her for a bit.'

Alone, Mrs Taylor stood up. *The Dumfries* had now vanished and her last cry was only heard by the one true God who accompanied her child to China and yet stayed by her side in her anguish.

Begin to trust

Louisa and Amelia were tramping around the cold Yorkshire countryside. Months ago they had both waved goodbye to Hudson and now they were frustrated at the lack of correspondence. But he was after all at the other side of the world and post was slow. So, to clear their minds and cheer themselves up, they had decided that a brisk walk was what they needed. Louisa and Amelia wandered along the lane to the local church yard. Amelia lifted up her skirts and sat on an old tomb stone in the corner. Louisa laughed out loud.

'Don't let the pastor see you do that, Miss Amelia Taylor. You'll cause a stir and the whole of Barnsley shall be talking about you!'

Amelia smiled, the very idea that she would cause a stir was almost laughable. It was more likely to be the flighty lass in front of her who would set people talking. But Louisa wasn't that bad. Maturity was setting in and occasionally Amelia caught a glimpse of it. Louisa was growing up. But though she was growing up, Amelia was still unsure about whether or not Louisa was converted. She wasn't a disgrace to their family or anything. Louisa was, as she described herself, 'independent and free thinking.'

Amelia never really quite knew what to make of her, her own sister. But Louisa was Louisa and as Amelia looked at her young sister, scrutinising her reflection in the church window, Amelia realised she wouldn't have her any other way. 'If only she knew the Lord,' Amelia murmured 'then I would simply breathe a sigh of relief.'

As they wandered home again Louisa asked if they could have another of their journal swapping sessions.

The logs crackled and spat as Louisa added some more on the fire. Then she brought out the box of old journals. Most belonged to Amelia, who didn't mind Louisa reading them any more. Whenever Louisa read something about herself she just laughed, she had a good sense of humour and it took a lot to offend her usually.

'I wonder if I shall find you writing about your infuriating sister again Amelia?' Louisa smiled mischievously.

'Hopefully not!' exclaimed Amelia. 'The last time was too embarrassing.'

Louisa stopped to think and then exclaimed, 'What I would like to read about is what happened after Hudson became converted.'

Amelia smiled, pleased at Louisa's interest in Hudson's conversion. A few times since Hudson's departure, on the 19th of September, last year, Louisa had tentatively asked questions about how Amelia had felt when Hudson had come to know the Lord, what exactly had it all meant? Perhaps this was another chance to reach out to her young sister. So Amelia had a brief rummage through the old journals before pulling one out.

'Read this one, I think this covers that period. We might get mother in later, once she has finished her visiting. She might have a journal to read to us too.'

Louisa picked up the journal and leafed through it. 'Hudson's departure seems a life time away now. It was sad that he left for China the day before your birthday.'

Amelia sighed as Louisa opened up the journal, and started to read. It was written when Amelia had been away at school.

I received a letter from Hudson today. Things are just the same as usual. Father gives medicine to rich and poor alike. To those who can't afford to pay, dear old father just says, 'It's all right we'll send the account to heaven and settle it there.' He never changes. He still goes on about China, which makes two fanatics in our family. Hudson and Father must drive poor Mother mad at times. Anyway Hudson seems to hit highs and then plummet to lows. He begins his letter enthusiastically enough,

Dearest Amelia,

I have been to see Mr Whitworth, our old Sunday school teacher. Do you remember him and his long whiskers? Well I remembered that he had connections with the British and Foreign Bible society. Who better to contact than him about getting a copy of the Chinese Scriptures. I paid him a visit and immediately he gave me a copy of the gospel of Luke in the Mandarin dialect. He also told me about a minister in Barnsley who can give me another book on China that I have not read yet. Apparently this book will give me some direction about the medical training I should receive before I go to China. However, as I progress with the gospel of Luke in Mandarin I realise that I am in much need of a Chinese dictionary and grammar book. Both are in fact necessary. However I do not have the twenty guineas required to purchase these books. Sometimes I wonder what use can I be to China, an uneducated chemist's son. I will try my best and can do no more.'

Louisa leafed through the pages again. 'Poor Hudson he worked so hard. Ah! Here is something Amelia. You must have written this a few weeks later.'

Hudson has made amazing progress. I couldn't believe it when I read his letter from Barnsley this morning. He has learnt 500 Chinese characters in the space of a few weeks.

Hudson and Father have explained to me in the past the strange way the Chinese write. It sounds incredibly difficult. To read and write in China must be so hard. You would have to be extremely clever. Every word in their language is called a character. Each character looks like a drawing. Each drawing stands for a different word. To put it into our context it's almost like having to learn hundreds and hundreds of letters before you would be able to start reading or writing. I am so thankful that I have only had to learn twenty-six letters. To hear Hudson describe his studies nearly exhausts me. Here I am, away at school and there he is studying his heart out at home, as well as working in the dispensary and searching here there and everywhere for any information on China that he can get his hands on. Hudson tells me that he has to get up at five in the morning to get all his studies done and so 'finds it necessary to go to bed early.'

No wonder. Five in the morning! I'd need to go to bed early if I was getting up at that time of the morning. His excuse is, as always, 'I must study if I am to go to China.'

Hudson can be stubborn. He concluded his letter by talking about China once again.

'I have decided to go, and am making every preparation I can. I intend to rub up my Latin, learn Greek and Hebrew, and get as much general information as possible.'

Oh Hudson! He will tire himself out if he is not careful!

Louisa flicked through pages that included many references to Marianne Vaughan.

'I remember her,' Louisa said roughly. 'High and mighty, hoity toity.'

'Louisa! Marianne is still my friend. She could not marry Hudson and that is the end of it. What do these journal entries say anyway?'

'Well here's one from that Christmas visit just after you had become "particularly friendly with darling Marianne".'

Amelia scowled at Louisa's sarcastic tone. Louisa now read out Hudson's descriptions of the young music teacher 'She is decidedly attractive.' 'Bright and gifted.' 'A voice so sweet it is a pleasure to listen to her.'

'Louisa,' Amelia snapped, 'give it to me. I shall read it in the way I wrote it.' Amelia snatched back the journal and began again.

Hudson could not be in love with a sweeter, more gentle young woman. Marianne and Hudson. The two people I like most in the world. Oh, and they would be so good for one another. Hudson would be a rock for Marianne to cling to, who would bring her continually closer to God and nurture her in her faith, and Marianne would look after him. I will not feel so worried about him leaving for a life in China if he has Marianne by his side. He will not be so lonely if she goes with him.

'Humph!' Louisa grunted. 'Romantic nonsense!'

'Louisa,' Amelia laughed, 'You're the worst romantic I know! Anyway let's continue. There's an entry a few months later. Yes, here it is. It's the day I heard that Hudson was going to be coming to Hull.'

Hudson replied to my letter this morning. It's so exciting. He is coming to live in Hull. He has managed to find a position with one of the busiest doctors in the whole of Hull. He will be an assistant and do all sorts of important work. The doctor is in actual fact Dr. Hardey, a brother-in-law to our aunt and seems to be just the thing Hudson requires to set him on his feet in the medical profession. He will require a lot of medical training if he is to go to China and anyway a medical training will not go wrong whatever happens. The most important thing is that Hull is within easy reach of Barton, which is where I live and where Marianne lives and I believe Hudson is happy to be within such easy reach of us both. He takes up the apprenticeship on his nineteenth birthday, which is just a matter of weeks now.

Louisa peered over her sister's shoulder. 'What was that like working in a doctor's surgery?'

Amelia looked up, 'It was busy. On his first day he didn't manage to write a letter until midnight. Amelia then brought out a small note.

It's midnight and I am at last at 13 Charlotte Street, Hull. This is a brief note to tell you about my new situation. From what I have seen of it, so far, I think I will like it exceedingly. I am to have an hour to myself at dinner and another at tea-time. I might be able to run over to Barton sometimes in the evening if I arrange things and am willing to stay overtime when needed. God has, up to now, granted all my prayers and he will grant me more before midsummer.

You understand.

Love, Hudson.

Louisa looked puzzled. 'Is that a coded message then? What did he mean by 'midsummer'?'

'Well,' admitted Amelia, 'He was probably referring to Marianne. When he put pen to paper he was always more discreet.'

'In case Mother or anyone should read it?'

'I suppose so. Marianne really hurt him I'm afraid. However, China was still his main concern. God had called him there and that was that.'

'Well what was Hull like then?' quizzed Louisa. 'It's ages since I've been there.'

'It's a fishing town really. It sits just where the River Hull joins the Humber. Hudson really enjoyed his time there. He was kept so busy. He dispensed medicines, kept accounts, dressed wounds, attended midwifery cases and even lectures at the medical school. Dr Hardey was attentive to Hudson's training and the two would even pray together in the surgery. It was in Hull that Hudson first heard of George Müller. Mr Müller has had quite an effect on Hudson.

'I must read you this extract. Hudson hadn't been in Hull long when he heard that an experienced missionary to China, a Mr Lobscheid, would be arriving in England. Hudson wanted to meet him. He arranged the meeting at the same time the Great Exhibition was running in London. Hudson got a whole week off work. He booked lodgings for us in Soho, London, and for my sixteenth birthday invited me to come to London for a whole week to attend the Great Exhibition and then meet Mr Lobscheid.

Louisa humphed again. 'I remember that. I was so jealous. London and the Great Exhibition.' Amelia smiled and handed Louisa the journal to read out loud.

What a day! I can hardly believe the activity that has taken place today. First thing we got up and had breakfast which was delicious. We both dressed warmly. There was a slight nip in the air this morning. Then we set off for the Great Exhibition. I had heard so much about this exhibition and was really excited about actually going to see it. Me, a young Yorkshire lass, visiting London. I could hardly believe it.

We eventually arrived at the glittering palace and it just took my breath away. If the truth be known I thought Piccadilly was amazing with all the people and noise but when I arrived at the Crystal Palace I knew I would never see anything like it again in all my days. It is a sight to behold with glass from top to bottom. It shines like diamonds glinting in the sun when you walk through Hyde Park.

We must have spent hours wandering round all the inventions and discoveries. Every labour saving device you can think of was there. Transport inventions were around every corner and amazing ways to communicate to people. Every idea under the sun was there from the sublime to the ridiculous. My head cannot contain them all.

The amount of people that thronged the palace was another spectacle to behold. I have never seen so many people and all in the same place. At first I felt quite lost and bewildered. Many people have come to the exhibition on the cheap excursion trains that have been laid on from almost every part of Britain. What a way to celebrate your sixteenth birthday.

But that wasn't all. It came to lunch-time and Hudson had another treat laid in store. We were to eat in style in a fancy restaurant. I could hardly believe it. I still have to pinch myself when I think of it now. We sat down at a table laid with silver cutlery. Hudson asked me what I would like to eat. I found this question a bit disturbing, as I am not used to having to choose what I want to eat. Ever since I was born, I have just eaten what was put in front of me. So Hudson decided to help me with one or two suggestions and then something caught his eye. I followed his gaze and saw the most amazing thing I had ever seen. It was far stranger than any invention and more dangerous looking than any of the machinery I had seen that morning. Fearfully I asked Hudson, 'What do you suppose it is and what do you think these people are going to do with it?'

Hudson sniggered as I watched. Two people, a gentleman and a lady, had this huge oval thing placed on the middle of their table. It was oval and yet it had spikes sticking out from all over it and a peculiar sprouting thing coming out of the top. Hudson hid behind his menu and whispered to me, 'Look Amelia, they are eating it!' I turned again and saw a waiter carving up what now appeared to be a very large and unusual fruit. I heard the woman exclaim, 'Oh, how lovely. A pineapple!' She had obviously eaten one before and enjoyed it or else she would not have reacted like that. Hudson looked at me and I looked at him. 'We can't afford it!' I gasped.

'Yes we can,' he said. 'Here it is on the menu. If we share it like that gentleman and his wife we will have enough money. I want to try this pineapple for myself.'

Hudson ordered the pineapple and we watched as it was cut into slices at the table. Hudson had been watching how the other couple ate the fruit and tucked in straight away. I watched him. His whole face lit up.

'Amelia,' he said 'there is nothing so sweet, so delicious as this pineapple. Words escape me. I can't describe how...' but I had already taken the plunge and was enjoying it for myself.

The taste of the sweet pineapple still on our lips, we left the exhibition to cross the crowded city, to the Bank of England. Hudson had arranged to meet a gentleman called George Pearse there. Mr Pearse is the Secretary of the Chinese Society and a member of the Stock Exchange. He has arranged for us to go with him next Sunday to Brook Street Chapel, Tottenham, where Hudson will finally be introduced to Mr Lobscheid. Mr Lobscheid may help Hudson in his plans to go to China.

Louisa interrupted her sister with 'So what was this Lobscheid like then?'

'Mr Lobscheid, Louisa, was peculiar, loud and red headed.'

Louisa laughed out loud. 'Is that what you have written in your journal? Amelia Taylor you'd better not let your mother hear that.'

'What shouldn't I hear?' Mrs Taylor bustled into the parlour and Amelia blushed. 'Oh, nothing Mother.'

'Now Amelia,' she said sternly.

'Well I was remembering that gentleman Hudson and I met after the Great Exhibition, Mr Lobscheid. I've written in my journal that I thought he was peculiar, loud and red headed. I then go on to say, that at first, Mr Lobscheid didn't think Hudson was suited to the Chinese mission.'

'He has certainly been proved wrong' said Mrs Taylor, slightly miffed.

Amelia explained, 'When he saw Hudson's fair hair and blue-grey eyes he said "They call me a 'red-headed barbarian devil'. The Chinese would run from you in terror. You could never get them to listen at all." Hudson just replied, coolly, "And yet, it is God who has called me, and he knows the colour of my hair and eyes." Mr Lobscheid soon changed his mind about Hudson.'

Mrs Taylor smiled as her mind flitted back to these early Hull days. 'It wasn't only Mr Lobscheid that Hudson impressed. He impressed me too with his commitment and endurance. Now what was that trouble we had with Aunt Hannah? It was when Hudson had to change his lodgings.

'You see, I had news from Hudson one day that he had to leave Dr Hardey's lodgings and move to Aunt Hannah's in Kingston square. The Hardeys had to give Hudson's room to a relative who needed it. The whole situation worked out quite well. Hudson was quite a help to Hannah and Richard. That was why Aunt Hannah was a bit upset when he decided to leave there too.'

'What was the problem?' asked Louisa.

'There was no problem as such. It was just a decision Hudson came to. He enjoyed Kingston Square and Richard and Hannah's large circle of friends were always calling in unexpectedly. Hannah runs quite an open house. Hudson loved the family atmosphere, especially when Amelia came to spend Sundays with them. However,

Hudson had been studying in his Bible and had been reading about giving one tenth of all your income to the Lord. He realised that his salary included the amount that was also given him to pay Aunt Hannah, for his board and comfortable lodgings.' Mrs Taylor stood up and walked to the door. 'The question was shouldn't he also tithe this? He did some calculations and worked out that, if he was to tithe his entire income as well as what he paid to Aunt Hannah for lodgings, he would not be able to live on what was left. Hudson looked elsewhere for lodgings that would prove less expensive. He found them and that was that. It was more important to obey God, than to live in comfort as far as Hudson was concerned...

...'Girls I've just thought, since we're all together this afternoon, perhaps we should write Hudson a letter from the three of us? But we have to make lunch first. Amelia can you lay the table?'

The Taylor household jumped back to life. For a while they put away their memories and journals and concentrated on the day to day job of running a household. But lunch and chores were soon over and Mrs Taylor entered the parlour with a basket of thread and buttons - a couple of journals tucked under her arm. Louisa clutched some writing paper and a pen.

'We'll write Hudson in a while Louisa, not just yet. Amelia can get on with some of that darning... Louisa, you read from my journal.' Mrs Taylor handed Louisa the journal indicating where she should start to read.

Hudson has written saying that he is now very settled in his new lodgings at 30 Cottingham Terrace. Mrs Finch appears to be a lovely Christian woman and her husband is at sea and hence is not home that much. It is not clear whether he is a Christian or not. But Hudson is pleased with his room, which he gets for three shillings a week. It has a fireplace, which Mrs Finch apparently polishes every day, a bed, chair and desk. Hudson says in his letter, that from out of his window he can watch kingfishers and herons fishing and water fowl nesting in the reeds of the stream that runs by just outside his window.

I am pleased that, so far, the situation seems to be working out well. But I must admit I was worried at first when he said that he was going to change his lodgings. Hannah was too. She was concerned he was not happy with them at Kingston Square or thought the price of their lodgings too expensive. I have received two or three letters from Hannah about this issue and have had to reassure her that Hudson was indeed very happy at their home but that there were other issues involved.

Hudson believes that he must begin to live in a way which will toughen him up a bit. Our home isn't the lap of luxury but I have to admit we are well off and Hudson has never lacked for anything. Further on in his letter Hudson says, 'My friends from church agree with me now that God is calling me to go to China as soon as possible. So now I have two main objectives. These are, to learn to endure hardships and to live cheaply. But don't worry about me mother, I shall be fine. My God will care for me.'

But I can't help but worry when I read something like that. All this talk about frugal living makes me a little uneasy. He boasts about eating special brown biscuits, which are as cheap as bread and much nicer. He eats these biscuits for breakfast with herring and black coffee. Why, he has even started making his own pickled cabbage. Then he talks about finding cheese for sale at four to six pence a pound. He goes on about it being better than some he had eaten at home for as much as eight pence. Now I am sure he is talking rubbish. There is no cheese better than Barnsley cheese and of that I am certain! But that's not a proper diet - brown biscuits, herring, pickled cabbage and cheese! And Amelia tells me that the rest of his money is being given away. He has admitted to her that it is as much as sixty per cent of his earnings! I worry about him. He only tells me half of it. Yet he swears to

Amelia that the more he gives away, the happier he is. In a letter to her he says, 'Unspeakable joy all the day long, and every day, is my happy experience. God is a living, bright reality; and everything I do is joyful service to him.'

How is he going to survive China? I think about it more and more each day. He will have no one out there. None to help him or see that he is properly fed. His only help will be his God. I should trust God more. God is more than enough help for anybody. Hudson closes his letter with this:

'Before I leave for China, where I shall be entirely dependant on God for all my daily needs, I must learn to move man, through God, by prayer alone.'

This is continually on his mind and I can see the wisdom of it. It is only God that can ultimately control man and he will meet Hudson's needs - he will provide for him in every way.

Mrs Taylor then remembered something. 'Thankfully God has shown us in the past just how well he can look after Hudson. Do you remember the fiasco about Hudson's wages?' Amelia sighed and nodded her head. Mrs Taylor continued. 'I didn't hear about all this when it was going on or I would have been down to Hull like a shot! Apparently Robert Hardey was in the habit of forgetting to give Hudson his wages. But usually, he wouldn't forget for too long and would pay up a day or two late. But this time, Hudson was desperately short of money and the days passed and there was no wages. He did not ask for help, that was typical of Hudson. He insisted on trusting God to provide. This was the only way he could prove that he was called to work in the much tougher atmosphere of inland China.

'Anyway, let me tell you the story. Hudson found that he had only one half crown piece left. It was everything he had. That evening as he sat, contemplating this desperate financial situation, a knock was heard at his door and a tall, well built man stood there holding his cap and looking anxious.

"Please sir," he said with a desperate edge to his voice. Hudson could tell from his accent the man was Irish and desperately worried. "Please sir, my wife is dying. Will you please come and pray with her?"

'Hudson was curious. Usually an Irish family would send for the priest to pray with the dying. So he asked the man why he hadn't sent for one. "I did send for the priest, sir." The husband replied. "But he refused to come without a payment of eighteen pence. I don't have enough - my family is starving."

'Hudson quickly agreed to come with the man, and grabbing his coat and bag, quickly left to follow the distraught man along the roads and back alleys to the draughty little dwelling he called home. As they walked along in the dark, both lost in their own thoughts, Hudson remembered his solitary half-crown. It was all he had and it was in one coin. He couldn't get change at this time of night, so couldn't even help the man with a little bit of money. And besides, back at his room Hudson had enough food for tomorrow's breakfast, but nothing more. "If only I had this half-crown in smaller change. I would gladly give these poor people a shilling."

'Hudson followed the man into a courtyard. Hudson remembered the courtyard. "I've been here before," he muttered to himself. "The last time I was here, a crowd of people grabbed my tracts and ripped them to pieces, promising to beat the living daylights out of me if I ever came here again." Anxiously he followed the man up a narrow flight of stairs into a dirty, damp room. Five sets of frightened, startled, eyes peered at him from behind a door. Looking harder Hudson noticed the hollow cheeks and lank hair. The children were malnourished.

'Hudson then heard the whimper of a new born baby in the next room. A very weak woman lay on the floor attempting to nurse a new born infant. Hudson looked at her and found himself saying, "Don't despair, there's a kind and loving Father in heaven." But he hated himself for saying it when he wasn't prepared to trust God for his own provisions and give the poor family his half-crown. Inwardly he chastised himself, "You hypocrite!"

'Turning to the man he said, "You asked me to pray with your wife." Hudson knelt down and prayed, "Our Father, who art in heaven." But at the same time his conscience scolded him, "How dare you kneel down and call God your Father with that half-crown in your pocket?"

'Hudson could hardly get through the prayer. The husband, holding his wife's hand in his, turned to Hudson and pleaded, "You see what a desperate state we are in, Sir. If you can help us, for God's sake, do."

'Hudson looked at the five hungry children, the newly born baby, the dying mother and he remembered the words of Matthew 5:42. "Give to the one who asks you." Putting his hand in his pocket Hudson took out the half crown. Quietly he said to the distraught father, "You may think that this is a small thing for me to do - to give you half a crown. But it is all the money I have. What I have been trying to tell you is true. God really is a Father, and you can trust him."

'Hudson left the husband, who had tears running down his cheeks and who was now telling his wife the tide had turned and everything was going to be all right, their prayers had been answered. God had looked out for them and brought them through. Walking through the courtyard, down the dark dimly lit streets and on up the dirty farm track to the little cottage, Hudson's heart was, as he said himself, "as light as his pocket". He sat down to a thin bowl of porridge and decided that he would not have swapped it for a prince's feast. "Dear God," he prayed as he knelt beside his bed. "Your word says that, he who gives to the poor lends to the Lord. Don't let the loan be a long one, or I shall have no lunch tomorrow!"

'Incidentally, the woman lived and the child was saved too. Hudson often thought afterwards that, had he not had the courage to trust God at that moment, his whole spiritual life would have been wrecked.'

Louisa was just about to interrupt her mother when Amelia stopped her. 'Wait a minute Louisa the story isn't finished yet.'

Mrs Taylor continued, 'The next morning, Hudson was eating his breakfast. The postman knocked at the door. Mrs Finch, the landlady came into the parlour and handed Hudson a letter. The handwriting on the envelope was unfamiliar and Mrs Finch's wet hands had smudged the postmark. Opening it he discovered a pair of kid gloves inside a blank piece of paper. Who was it from? Hudson had no idea. He looked at the gloves. They were nice gloves and would keep his hands quite warm. Just then something fell out from inside one of the gloves, hit the floor and rolled off under the table. Hudson got down on his hands and knees to retrieve the wayward object. Grabbing hold of it, he almost bumped his head on the dining table in his surprise. A gold half sovereign lay shining in his hand.

"A whole gold half sovereign! I can hardly believe my own eyes. Praise the Lord! Four hundred percent for just twelve hours' investment. Now that is good interest! How glad the merchants of Hull would be if they could lend their money at such a rate!" Hudson remembered a phrase that he had heard George Müller use once to describe the kingdom of God, "The bank that will not break". Hudson decided that "The bank that would not break" would have all his money from that moment on. "If we are faithful in little things," he concluded "we shall gain experience and strength that will be helpful to us in the more serious trials of life."

'Hudson's faith was boosted, but the ten shillings didn't last for ever and, so, he kept praying for the larger sum that he needed. But none of his prayers seemed to be answered. Ten days after receiving the half sovereign, he was in almost the same scrape as before.

"Dear God, please remind Dr Hardey that my salary is overdue," he prayed urgently.

'It was not only a question of money for Hudson. Hudson felt that he had to prove that he could depend totally on God. After all, that was the situation he was going to be in when he left for China. Hudson felt he must rely totally on prayer, on telling his Heavenly Father what he had need of and then trusting that God would see to it.

'Many people might say that that was foolish of him. You would be right to say that he was entitled to his salary and should have simply gone up to Dr Hardey and demanded the salary there and then. He would have been within his rights and it would not have been a sin for him to have done that. But Hudson wanted to be sure that he was totally fit for a life of complete surrender to God. He saw this situation as a vital test to pass. Could he trust God completely?

'It would have been so easy for him to have asked the doctor for his salary. But instead Hudson felt he should rest in God and wait for his provision. China would not be an easy place to live because, although he would be supported by the missionary society and by contributions from home, he could not depend on receiving this money regularly.

'On Saturday morning Hudson sat on the edge of his bed, chewing his nails and sending up prayers, like a bombardment of arrows. At the end of the day he had to give Mrs Finch the rent for that month's accommodation. "Should I ask Dr Hardey for the salary? Just a quick word in his ear and it would all be over and Mrs Finch will not have to wait for her rent payment. She needs the money too. I do not want her to do without a single penny on my account." He prayed once more and seemed to get an answer straight from God, 'Wait. My time is best.' So he waited and went to work that day quite relaxed.

'At about five o'clock that afternoon, Hudson was with Dr Hardey in the surgery writing up the last of the prescriptions. With the last prescription dealt with, Dr Hardey threw himself back in his arm chair with a sigh of contentment. "Another week gone by Hudson, eh? Time flies, as they say, especially in a doctor's surgery."

'Hudson nodded, one eye on the doctor in his chair and the other on a pan of medicine he was heating up on the stove. Hudson nearly knocked the pan off the stove in shock at what he heard next. The doctor coughed and muttered, "Oh by the way Hudson, surely your salary should be due shortly? I shall have to get that organised." Hudson swallowed a couple of times before replying as nonchalantly as possible, "It has been overdue for some time."

'Dr Hardey sat up in his chair. "Why didn't you say something? You should remind me. I am sorry that has happened. I wish I had thought of it sooner." The doctor looked flushed and very vexed. "Why only this afternoon I sent all the money I had to the bank. Otherwise I would have paid you this instant. As it happens now I shan't be able to pay you until the banks open again on Monday."

'Hudson felt sick! His legs felt as though they should give way at any moment. Just when he thought God had sorted it all out and that he would be able to give Mrs Finch her money as promised, everything went wrong. It was as if someone had pulled the rug out from beneath Hudson's feet and sent him flying in all directions. Just then the pan began to boil furiously and Hudson had to grab it and run out of the room. This was fortunate, for as soon as he was out of the room and laying the pan down on a safe surface, tears crept into his eyes. Hudson clenched his fist and forced his emotions back inside. He did not want the doctor to see him like this. "God help! God help!" he cried. After that quick prayer he felt better and more composed. His hands had stopped shaking which meant he could pour the, now cooling, medicine into a dispensary bottle. He knew God would not fail him.

'The rest of the evening was spent in the surgery, reading his Bible and preparing some talks. At ten o'clock Hudson put on his overcoat and put away his notes. One look at the clock told him how late it was and that Mrs Finch would now be in bed. He would have to let himself in with his own key and perhaps tomorrow he would ask her if he could pay early next week instead. It wasn't ideal, but it would have to do.

'Just as Hudson was about to turn out the surgery lights and clear up one or two last bits and pieces, he heard Dr Hardey's footsteps almost dancing up the garden path. "Hudson Taylor! You'll never guess what has happened." Dr Hardey rushed into the surgery holding a fist full of bank notes in one hand and a pouch full of sovereigns in the other. "Get the ledger boy I am going to have to do a little bit of last minute accounting tonight. Take these!" With that Dr Hardey shoved a handful of notes into his hand. "My richest patient decided to pay up his bill tonight and in cash! Can you believe it? I've never known him to pay in cash before. He always pays by cheque. Most business men round here do. He always pays his bills when he comes for a check up. He never makes a special visit. Until tonight that is!" The doctor held his sides as the laughter almost ached inside him. "I am so glad I can pay you tonight. It has been bothering me so much!" Hudson laughed too and tears of relief ran down his face. The doctor just thought his young assistant was enjoying the joke as much as he was and didn't realise how desperate a situation Hudson had been in.

'As Hudson left the surgery that night he felt as if he

were walking on air. "Praise God. I can go to China after all! I have passed the test. I trusted in God and he did not fail me." A whoop of joy escaped from Hudson's heart. It echoed and re-echoed off the high tenement buildings as he made his way back to Drainside. An old man flung up his window and yelled at him "Be quiet you young rogue!" Hudson clammed up instantly, apologised profusely but still skipped the rest of the way home.'

'That was a good story!' exclaimed Louisa.

'I do wish we had another letter though,' sighed Amelia.

'Well we don't Amelia, but we can write. Where's your pen and paper Louisa, let's begin.'

The Storm begins

Later that evening, Mrs Taylor leafed through a pamphlet they had received that morning from the Chinese Evangelisation Society. It was called the CES for short. They were the society that Hudson had joined and he depended on them for financial assistance. They certainly weren't the most organised of missionary societies and would cause Hudson one or two problems in the future. Not long after the CES had announced their plans, to send missionaries to China, Hudson Taylor had booked a ticket from Hull to London. Hudson had felt that he must further his medical training if he was to be of any use in a Chinese situation. Amelia had waved him off, crying her eyes out and looking as pretty as a picture in her pink floral dress. Hudson, according to Amelia, had looked so severe and grown-up as he set off into the unknown of London.

'Help us all,' thought Mrs Taylor as she remembered, 'He's in China now and back then we were worrying about him being in London!'

In London he had learnt dissection. Due to some carelessness on his part he caught malignant fever from an infected corpse. His colleagues were angry with him for working on a dead body with a cut finger. Hudson, as determined as ever said, 'There is nothing to worry about.

Unless I am greatly mistaken I have work to do in China and I shall not die. But if I don't recover then I will look forward to going to be with my master.' Unfortunately, Hudson had to come home for rest and recuperation. He had his usual money problems. His old landlady had been in a spot of bother financially and asked Hudson if he could get word to her husband, who was on board a ship, that she needed his wages now. Hudson decided to help her out and immediately gave her money from his own salary. However, Mrs Finch's husband was nowhere to be found and so Hudson ended up with no money at all. However, God looked after Hudson and Mr Finch was located. Hudson eventually had the money he needed to get back to Barnsley.

Mrs Taylor sighed as she lifted up another pair of socks to darn. She thought about poor Hudson recovering from the fever.

'Maybe it wasn't so much of "poor Hudson" after all,' she thought. 'Marianne Vaughan rushed to his bedside and they were soon engaged. Hudson was overjoyed. He was finally engaged to the woman he loved. But it didn't last long of course.'

Mrs Taylor rummaged in her basket for some thread. 'The engagement fell apart at the seams, Hudson left for China, and now he has been away for so many months and all we have are one or two letters. Never mind, perhaps tomorrow will bring us some news, or the next day? We shall trust God, day by day.'

When the last of the sewing was completed, Mrs Taylor put the guard over the fire, turned down the lamp and went to bed.

***

The following morning Amelia and Louisa sat in the bedroom - reading one of Hudson's letters. It had been months since it had arrived and seemed like their only connection with him.

'Read some to me, Amelia, please,' Louisa pleaded as she lay sprawled across the patchwork quilt on the bed. 'I want to hear it again, go on.'

'Very well. He starts by describing the voyage.' Amelia sat up straight and read in a steady, clear voice.

We faced the worst weather in the whole voyage in the first twelve days before we hit the open sea. Thinking back on it now, these dangers we faced, between the Irish and Welsh coasts, could very well have been the evil one, trying to send me to the bottom of the ocean.

'What on earth does he mean?' Louisa's brow was wrinkled in thought.

Amelia sighed, 'Well he means that the Devil was trying to stop him. As a Christian you are in conflict with the Devil. His aim is to destroy the kingdom of God, only, he can never do it. God is mightier and none can overcome his power.'

Amelia thought for a second or two and then added, 'I can quite understand the Devil wanting to stop Hudson getting to China. There are many people who will hear about Jesus Christ for the first time, simply because Hudson has had the courage to follow God's call there. God will use Hudson mightily, of that I am sure.'

'So Hudson thinks the Devil was about to drown him in the Irish channel then?' Louisa's tone was slightly sarcastic. Her strong-minded nature was coming out and she was ready for an argument.

But Amelia wasn't having that! 'Yes! I believe Hudson is under attack by the Devil. But don't be so flippant about it. He could easily have died during that crossing. The ocean is a dangerous place, where men lose their lives daily. Without God's protection Hudson could very well have been lost at sea and not even seen China.'

'But he's there now!'

Amelia thought better of continuing the argument and calmed down. 'That's true Louisa. Next Hudson describes the storm.'

We were, in fact, two boat's length from being smashed to pieces on the rocks. The fearful wind had driven us into Carnarvon Bay and the scene at midnight was of huge foaming breakers crashing all around us. It was a fearful time. The wind was blowing terrifically, and we were tearing along at a frightful rate - one moment high in the air and the next plunging head first through the waves, as if we were about to go to the bottom of the ocean.

One side of the ship was fearfully high, while the other side was quite low. At times the sea could be seen flooding over onto the ship. In this utter chaos, I watched the bright red sun setting beyond the horizon. It was beautiful in its ferocity. As I was more help out of the way of the ship's crew, I retired quickly to my cabin, soaked through and shivering.

That night I slept very little. I curled up in my bunk bed and worried about you all hearing that I had drowned off the coast of Wales. I worried about the money that had been spent by the missionary society on my ticket to Shanghai - it cost them nearly £100. Then I worried about the crew who were not ready to die and what it would be like to drown beneath the waves. It was not a pleasant night. To comfort myself I read one or two hymns, some psalms and then John chapters thirteen through to fifteen. The situation worsened throughout the next day as we tried to clear land. However, the wind was against us continually, driving us nearer to the rocks.

I wrote my name in my pocket book, along with our address in Yorkshire, and secured this in my jacket pocket. I fully expected to be swept overboard and my name and address would have helped in the identifying of my body.

However, just when we were sure we were lost, the Captain steered the ship away from the rocks. Praise God!

Louisa's eyes were as large as saucers at this true life adventure. Amelia felt chilled to the bone. It was all too close for comfort. This was her brother, two ship lengths from death and drowning. It didn't bear thinking about. 'Thankfully mother gave him a swimming belt. If the boat had sunk he would have floated with that!' Louisa said cheerfully.

Hudson had neglected to mention that, at the peak of the danger he had given away his swimming belt to another sailor. But Louisa and Amelia did not know this. If they had they would have been furious with him!

'Read on, Amelia, what does he say next?'

'Well the next bit is from the Bay of Biscay.' Amelia continued reading.

I have just discovered another Christian on board! He is Swedish and together we plan to ask the Captain's permission to hold regular Bible teaching and worship among the crew.

Amelia filled in Louisa with the rest of their brother's evangelistic efforts on board *The Dumfries*.

'He says the crew are not interested in giving their lives to Christ. But some will have private chats and prayer with him. He says that some appear very near the kingdom though unwilling to make the final step and come out fully on the side of Christ. The next bit is quite difficult.' Amelia's voice trembled as she began.

How widely we are separated. It was not so long ago that we were so close, so near to each other. But Praise God - he is unchangeable, his mercy never fails.

I was reading today the following verse from a hymn, 'I give thee to thy God, The God that gave thee.' The last time I sang this I sang it with Mother - after which she broke down in tears, at the thought of our parting. May the Lord bless her and comfort her day by day. The love of Christ is everything. As much as I long to see you all, the love of Christ is stronger. I cannot fight it.

Amelia wiped a tear from her eye and then read on.

Some weeks ago we rounded the Cape of Good Hope and have just sailed past countless numbers of islands, some densely populated, all of them with people who have not heard the good news of Jesus Christ. How is it that Christians can sit at home in their comfortable chairs and leave these lost people to perish?

'Hudson then goes on to describe some further weather problems.' Amelia knelt down beside Louisa to show her the letter. 'However, this time instead of too much wind there is too little and the ship is slowly drifting towards some sunken reefs.'

The captain came to me on the deck and said, 'Well we have done everything that can be done. We can only await the result.' Just then a thought occurred to me and I replied, 'No, there is one thing we have not done yet!'

'What is that?' he queried.

'Four of us on board are now Christians. Let us each retire to his own cabin, and pray to the Lord to give us immediately a breeze. He can send one, I know he can!'

The Captain agreed and straightaway all four Christians retired to pray. I, immediately, went on my knees to ask God for a breeze and soon I knew my prayer had been heard and that a breeze was now on its way! Quickly I rushed out on deck and bumped into the first officer. He is a godless man and quite an awkward one too. I asked him to let down the mainsail which had been drawn up in the absence of any wind. The first officer looked at me incredulously and muttered, 'Now what would be the good of that!' I told him that we had been asking for a wind from God and that it was coming immediately. 'We are so near the reef there is not a moment to lose,' I urged. With a look of contempt he said he would rather see wind than hear of it. But while he was speaking I watched his eye, following it up to where the topmost sail was beginning to tremble in the breeze.

'Look!' I exclaimed. 'Now you see!'

'Phsaw! That's merely a cat's paw.' Sailor's talk for the slightest puff of wind.

But he let the mainsail down anyway and the Captain came up to see what was the matter. In a few minutes we were ploughing our way through the water and were soon passing the Pelew Islands. God does answer prayer and gives the help each emergency requires!

Louisa stared at the letter, enthralled. 'How amazing! What adventures! Go on Amelia, what's next.'

Amelia cleared her throat. 'He now arrives in China.'

How lonely I am. There is not one single person that I know here. I am quite alone.

It just came over me all of a sudden when I left the crew on *The Dumfries* and arrived at last in Shanghai. There was not one hand held out to welcome me. Not one person knows my name.

Amelia's hand trembled as she held the letter. Every time she read it, it hurt her, painfully. Louisa grasped Amelia's hand. 'I should not have asked you to read it again. I know how it hurts you.'

'Does it not hurt you Louisa?' Amelia asked sharply.

Louisa ignored the barbed words and replied quietly, 'Yes, it does hurt me but then I realise that he wrote this letter ages ago. He's bound to have made friends by now. We might even get another letter, in a few days, which tells us that he now knows the whole of Shanghai and is going away to find some peace and quiet.'

Amelia laughed. 'Shanghai isn't like Barnsley. It's bigger than Hull even. But you are right I think. He will have made friends by now. I just wish we could hear some more news, that's all.'

'Yes, I know. We'll get a letter soon. Don't you worry.'

Just then there was a knock on the door. Mr Taylor went to answer it. Amelia and Louisa dropped what they were doing and leaned their heads over the bannister to see who was calling. There was nobody there. Just then Mr Taylor skipped back into the parlour.

'You shall never guess what I have!' he exclaimed breathlessly.

The girls rushed down the stairs. He held in his hands a pile of...

'LETTERS!'

The cry went up from Amelia, Louisa and Mrs Taylor all at once.

'Yes, my darlings. Letters and lots of them.'

That morning was spent reading and re-reading

month's worth of Hudson's letters. What a luxury, a whole bunch of letters at once.

'It was a long wait,' thought Amelia, 'but it was worth it, just to see his hand writing again and know that he is alive. God thank you, thank you.'

The Letters Begin

Hudson's letters were read and re-read many times that day and throughout the following weeks.

Among the first things that I have had to do is find a house, establish financial arrangements with the CES and learn enough of the Chinese language and customs to be able to manage on my own. On my first Sunday afternoon I went into the city. You will have heard that Shanghai is under siege. I walked around the outside of the city wall and saw row after row of wrecked houses and the misery of the people who have had to flee their homes. Some rebel soldiers were guarding the city and we spoke to them. All were dressed in red scarves, rich silk coats with bright lapels and green silk trousers.

I managed to speak, in Chinese, to some people and I gave away tracts. I even got some temple priests to listen to the gospel and they too took some tracts away with them.

However, at the North gate of the city, I saw some fierce fighting. One man was brought in dead and another had been shot through the chest. I examined a third man and found that a cannon ball had gone right through his arm. The arm was severely broken and he was writhing in agony. I urged his colleagues to take him to the hospital immediately, for there was nothing I could do for him, as I did not have the necessary equipment with me.

There is not much I can do to stop men fighting. I can only bring them the good news of the gospel of peace. I must admit though, I do find it hard when I see a group of soldiers dragging prisoners along by their pigtails. The prisoners call out to me to save them, but I can do nothing.

That sounds awful, murmured Amelia as she picked up another letter. 'What does this one say?'

I am very well provided for here, though the finances I receive from CES are sporadic and much less than the other missionaries receive.

Unfortunately, when I unpacked some of my cases I discovered that ink bottles had burst over many of my books and papers. My shoes too have been ruined. But I still have much to be thankful for. I have arrived safely and am about to embark on God's calling for my life.

Mrs Taylor picked up another letter to read out loud.

A quick note to tell you that I am well and that the fighting is over. The British and Americans have come ashore. With their flags flying and drums beating they marched on the imperialist troops who surrounded the city.

There have been repercussions for us missionaries however. It appears that the imperialists are angry with us as we are foreigners, and therefore, associated with their defeat. It will be many months now before we can go out into the country-side to preach.

Another letter quickly followed that one.

Thank you, thank you, thank you. I received your letter today, Mother. You must have sent it not long after I left Liverpool. Reading it has brought tears to my eyes, but please don't worry. I do get lonely here. Sometimes, I wish for nothing more than a wife to love me and care for me.

Before I left home I wrote to Elizabeth Sissons and it appears that she is very interested in China. I feel that I should mention her to you, as I am thinking that perhaps she may be interested in coming out to China. Before I left, some said, that she did in fact love me. Ask father to write. I do miss him.

How is Marianne? Is she well? I think of her often. She may get a richer and handsomer husband than I but I question whether she will get one who is more devoted.

Mrs Taylor sighed. Amelia looked awkward. Louisa looked at her Father and asked who this Elizabeth Sissons was and was she the sort that would be suitable for their Hudson. Mrs Taylor continued to read the letters. He was so far away, her young son, in need of advice, encouragement and a warm hug. That night she prayed long and hard that every need of her son's would be met. He was skimping and saving for the basics of life, but money wasn't what he needed most. Hudson was lonely and she hated thinking about that.

Other letters told the family about the house that he had moved into.

It's a wooden house near Shanghai's north gate and has twelve rooms. I am living upstairs and have had all the rooms cleaned and whitewashed. One room is my bedroom and another a dining room and study. The downstairs rooms are a dispensary, school room and chapel for the local Chinese. Today was the first day for my new school. Ten boys and five girls came. The dispensary is now busy too. Every day I have new patients. I have learnt all the necessary words to explain to my patients how they should take their medicines. It is vital that they understand. Misunderstandings are so common here when one is just beginning to learn Chinese.

There were many things Hudson didn't tell his family in his letters. He neglected to tell them that the area he was living in was in fact so dangerous that it had to be cut off at night from the rest of the international settlement. Hudson kept a night-light burning in his room while he slept and a swimming belt was close to hand. It was quite possible that, should trouble arise, Hudson would have to jump out his window into the water below and make his escape by swimming.

Mrs Taylor knew that Hudson would have to face many trials in the years ahead. As the letters continued to trickle in, she sympathised with some of them.

Dear Hudson,

Thank you for telling me about, your friend, John Burdon. We will pray for him. To lose a wife at any time is a hard cross to bear, but to lose her when you are so far away from home. You do well to comfort him. I am sorry to hear that there is still fighting in your locality. We worry about you, but know that you are safe in the care of our Lord. Your letter arrived this morning. What a joy to hear that you have three thousand Chinese New Testaments to hand out. I hope your journey into the Chinese interior goes well. It shall be some time before we hear from you but we shall be praying for you.

Dear Mother,

I have returned safely. Our journey went well. We hired a junk, which is a type of boat the locals use to transport goods and people up and down the river. We, however, were loaded down with New Testaments, medicine, clothes and bedding.

The tide was not in our favour and we had to abandon the junk and continue on foot. We visited many villages and communities along our route, preaching and looking for people who could read. Contrary to popular opinion not every Chinese man can read, but there are some, perhaps more than you might find in many European countries.

In Songjiang we made straight for the Buddhist temples. These are the normal places for public gathering. We drew quite a crowd and many followed us into the temple. My friend, Edkins, preached. I handed out the leaflets. Shaven-headed priests, in yellow robes, looked on, but did not try to stop us.

However, as we left the city, a crowd of men and boys began to jostle us. We turned down a side street to what we thought might be a ferry pier where we could get on board a junk and sail away. The men were quite threatening. As we got to the end of the pier, we realised that there were no boats available. We were trapped. The crowd cheered with delight as they closed around us. Boats passed by the pier and refused to stop and help us when they saw the crowd.

With one leap I jumped off the pier onto a passing boat. Quickly I tossed Edkins a rope which he used to pull the boat in towards the bank. Thankfully he managed to jump on too. The disgruntled boat owners dropped us off further on down the river. But the crowd caught us up. We were in a very precarious situation and would have been severely beaten, if not killed, were it not for a Chinese friend of mine, who just happened to be living in the city. It was quite incredible. I had hired him some months back as a language teacher and then dismissed him. Thankfully he did not resent me and managed to calm the crowd down. With my friend's help we were both escorted to safety and continued with our tract distribution.

There are so many people in these outlying areas who have not heard about the Lord Jesus Christ. Many eagerly listen to this message of hope that we bring. One high ranking ruler came to sit by us holding his crystal globe, which instantly told us he was a very important character. He lowered his voice and said to me, 'Your books are true. Your words are truth.' Then he left before we could speak to him some more.

I must say that the future looks promising. I plan to go tomorrow and buy an old boat that I have seen for sale. If I kit it out with furniture we will perhaps be able to use this boat for many more journeys and adventures like this one.

The letters continued to come. Many were sent to the whole family. Amelia loved nothing better than when she got a letter addressed to her, 'Miss Amelia Taylor.' She would disappear to a quiet spot to read it in private.

Dear Amelia,

I have just returned from another of my adventures.

John Burdon and I decided to hire two junks and sail to the point where the Yangtze estuary narrows away from the sea. We instructed our boatmen to enter the nearest inlet so that we could climb the mountains on the northern shore.

The countryside round there is exceptionally fertile. There is always a fresh breeze to cool your face. Everywhere that the eye can see there are fields of flowering peas and beans. The land is lush and green - a delight to the eyes. When we disembarked we counted five mountain peaks and noticed that the highest was topped with a fine, newly painted, pagoda. This is an ornate oriental building and quite extraordinary. Nestling at the foot of the hill and running up its slope was a Buddhist temple and monastery. Flowers and grass covered the mountainside, trees grew up from between the rocks, giving much needed shade. The area was very pleasant looking indeed. I particularly noticed the incredible colours. Take for instance the incredible deep colours of the cypress tree leaves. Then there is the beautiful sight of light graceful willows that mingle with orange, tallow and other trees. At each turn new shrines and pavilions met us. Eventually we arrived at the temple where a team of workmen were busy gilding the exterior. A festival was in full swing. The air was thick with the scent of incense and the streets were buzzing with activity. People threw coins into baskets, music sounded out from a hundred different instruments. Conversations were being held on every street corner and above all that noise was the tramp, tramp, tramp of a thousand feet.

A priest came up to me and asked me to kneel on a stool in front of his Buddha. I refused and warned them of the foolishness of idolatry. I told them that God loved them and that if anything that I said was contrary to the truth, then they should speak up. John preached to them in the Shanghai dialect. No one objected, then we moved on.

Our next stop was the city of Tongzhou. This is a notorious place called 'Satan's Seat'. John and I were well prepared for a difficult time. This town always gives foreigners a rough reception. Our two Chinese teachers tried to persuade us not to go. The town is well-known for its unruly mobs.

On the morning of our departure for Tongzhou, we instructed our Chinese friends to stay behind in the boats. 'If we don't return tonight,' I said, 'try to find out what has happened to us, then return as quickly as possible to Shanghai in one of the boats to tell the others. Leave the other boat behind in case we do manage to return. We will then be able to follow you on to Shanghai.

Leaving the teachers behind we departed with one servant. However, it wasn't long before our servant asked if he too could return. Tongzhou has an incredible reputation. Just then a respectable looking man approached us and said, 'I beg you not to enter the town. If you do, you will find to your sorrow what Tongzhou people are like.'

John replied, 'We are very grateful for your advice, but our minds are quite made up.'

At that our servant announced that he would go no further and ran back in the direction of the junk. I had to search around the surrounding villages for another man who would agree to the job. I had to pay him quite a hefty sum.

As we approached the West gate of Tongzhou, a huge bulk of a man approached us. He was very drunk and very angry. Grabbing John, by the shoulders, he began to shake him violently. John tried to get him off but just then a dozen violent-looking men arrived and we were both carried off into the city.

'Take me to the chief magistrate,' I yelled.

'We know what to do with your sort,' laughed one man.

As they carried us along the road, I worked out that they had, in fact, mistaken us for rebel soldiers. Suddenly the large drunk man dropped John in a heap and made a grab for me instead. He knocked me to the ground several times, pulled my hair and gripped my arms until they were black and blue.

During this time, John was still giving out leaflets at any opportunity. He would pull one out of his pocket and throw it at someone who would pick it up and read it out of pure curiosity. Eventually a squabble broke out.

'Take them to the magistrate.'

'Kill them now.'

I remembered that the apostles rejoiced when they were counted worthy to suffer for the cause of Christ. But, finally, I managed to get my hand into my pocket to bring out my identity card. This is just a sheet of red paper that has my name printed on it. After this they treated us both with more respect.

I ordered the men to take us to the chief official. When we arrived we were totally exhausted and drenched with sweat. My tongue stuck to the roof of my mouth and when the crowd let us go I fell in a heap on the floor. I asked for water. We were curtly told, 'You wait!' Eventually we were ushered into the presence of 'The Great and Venerable Father Chen'. Everyone fell on their knees when he entered the room. John and I refused on principle.

Thankfully 'The Great and Venerable Father Chen' was astute enough to realise that mistreating foreigners was not very wise. He treated us with the utmost courtesy. We gave him a New Testament. This he gratefully received, before serving us tea and refreshments.

As an apology, for the shocking way we had been treated in his town, he let us carry on with our tract distribution. We had full protection from his guards and eventually left the city with a team of runners to clear the way ahead of us. At one point I even saw these men clear a path through the undergrowth by using their long pig-tails as whips. I couldn't help but note the difference between our entering and leaving the very same city. Quite extraordinary.

'Quite extraordinary indeed Hudson', Amelia muttered. 'I don't think I will read this letter to mother. It wouldn't be wise.'

***

Mrs Taylor worried enough without hearing all the details of her son's adventures. She worried that he wasn't eating enough, that he had sounded depressed in his last letter, that they hadn't had a letter in quite a few months. Then another letter would arrive the following week and everything would be fine once again.

I spent my twenty-third birthday on Qindaosha Island. I am now eating all my meals with chopsticks. This is the start of a new direction for me. For some time, as I have lived amongst these people, preaching to them and bringing the gospel to them, I have noticed that they think I am a very peculiar creature indeed. I think I should perhaps attempt to become more like them. Perhaps my appearance has been a barrier to them in receiving the gospel. If they think I am ridiculous then perhaps they think my message is ridiculous as well. I will think about this some more as I am not quite sure how to go about it.

The boatsman that took me across to Qindaosha is delighted that I am now eating with chopsticks and he suggested that I have my head shaved and wear Chinese clothes. Another boatsman said that would look much better than the stupid stuff I wear now but he expressed regret that I cannot change my eyes or my nose. He thinks that these are the strangest bits about me.

You will be pleased to know that I have bought a cat and two kittens. The mice and rats, at home in Shanghai, have increased so much that I can no longer manage to control them myself. The rats are so cheeky they even eat my candles and jump onto my bed, when I am still in it!

There is a family of young girls that live down the road. Each one of them reminds me of Amelia and Louisa in some way. I am still thinking of Elizabeth. But there is one problem. I will never be able to marry until I can rely on the missionary society to send regular support.

Then another letter which held tragic as well as joyful news. Hudson was now living in Ningbo and a missionary's son had fallen ill with a life threatening fever. They had to get back to Shanghai.

Dear Mother,

I am writing again in haste. John Burdon's young son has just died. It appears our frantic rush from Ningbo back to Shanghai was in vain. The child was sick with a fever for a further three weeks after our return and he died only yesterday. John is very upset. He has now lost his wife and a child.

Yet I have good news to give you which will cheer you up immensely. In my last service, which I gave at our little Shanghai church, I asked a question not expecting to receive any answer.

'Jesus died for you and has taken the punishment. He has atoned for your guilt. Have any of you prayed to God and asked him to pardon your sins?'

'I have,' said Guihua, the young cook.

He is, Mother, our first convert in China. If one soul is worth worlds have I not been abundantly repaid, and you also, for all that you have given to the Lord and his work.

***

One morning Amelia rushed into her bedroom. Louisa had scarves, ribbons and garments all over the place.

'What do you think Amelia?' she asked, flouncing around in some outfit or other. 'Do you think it looks like that dress I saw in Hull?'

'Not a bit!' retorted Amelia. 'Forget dresses for a minute and listen to this. Hudson has sent a letter.'

Amelia began to read Hudson's letter.

I have long wanted to give the Chinese the courtesy of dressing, speaking and living like them all the time. Some friends however think this would be disgraceful behaviour.

However, I have made my decision and by the time you get this letter I will be wearing Chinese clothes and a big black pigtail called a bianzia. I have now dyed my hair. This wasn't as easy as I at first thought. I had to concoct the dye myself. But I also have had to grow my hair to a considerable length so as to be able to plait it. When concocting the dye I took a large bottle of ammonia and unscrewed the top. Unfortunately I did not realise that an immense pressure had built up inside the bottle. When I unscrewed the top the contents of the bottle burst out into my face. The chemical spurted into my nose and eyes, down my mouth, and all over my face and hair. Fumes from the escaped chemical were breathed into my lungs. I was in a bad way. I ran for my life hardly able to see. Somehow, I found my way to the kitchen and a bucket of cold water. Plunging my head into this bucket saved my life. Soon I found that I had the power to speak again and I yelled, 'Fetch Doctor Parker, quickly!'

Doctor Parker says that when he arrived my face was so swollen he could hardly recognise me. He quickly applied castor oil to my eyes and face, and gave me a large dose of pain killers. My feet were plunged into some hot water and ice was applied to my face and I was swiftly put to bed. Thankfully I have lived to tell the tale. Yesterday I went to a Chinese barber who completed the job. I now have a jet black pigtail and the rest of my head is shaved. That's how we wear our hair in China.

My clothes will be a much more pleasurable experience. Let me describe my wardrobe to you. Louisa will in no doubt be very interested in this.

Louisa squeaked in protest, but Amelia continued.

First I have socks to put on. These are made of calico and have thick stitched soles. Then there are some enormous breeches called han ku. These are, in fact, two feet too wide for me round the waist but, if I fold them in a certain way, I can, with a little bit of work, keep them up with a strong girdle. The legs remind me slightly of a large pair of bloomers. These I tuck into the socks just below the knee and this is all kept in place with a couple of coloured garters. Then there is a cotton shirt and on top of this I wear a colourful silk gown with wide sleeves that reach twelve or fifteen inches beyond the tips of my fingers. Finally, I have a pair of cloth shoes with upcurled toes. These are big enough to leave quite a bit of room for the bulky socks. Doctor Parker says that my breeches are big enough to store a fortnight's provisions in.

But today as I walked around the city no one even guessed that I was not Chinese. It was only when I began to distribute the literature that people realised who and what I was. The main difference that I have noticed is that the women and children are much more willing to come for medical treatment. They seem more at ease. They trust me.

Louisa sat on the edge of her bed, surrounded by her ribbons and petticoats. They held no interest for her now. Her mouth was open wide, her eyes agog. The picture she held in her mind was almost unbelievable.

Amelia didn't know what to make of it either.

Louisa blurted out, 'He needs a wife!'

Love's Beginning

Amelia sat on top of the old stone dyke that ran round one of the local farmer's fields. She'd received another letter from Hudson. It had been quite a few months since she had replied to his letter telling her about the colourful bloomers and the pigtail. She had also told Hudson that she was on the verge of getting married herself. She had written to Hudson just the other week.

Benjamin Broomhall is a good friend of us both Hudson. I know you will be happy for us.

Hudson's letters continued to come. The adventures never seemed to stop.

Dear Amelia,

William Burns and I have returned from our travels. One stop we made was, at Nanxun, just south of the Great Lake. We had heard that an immoral play was to be performed outside the city and that a vast camp of people had gathered to watch. Burns jumped onto the stage and stopped the play. He shouted, 'What you are doing is very wrong. This behaviour will land you in hell.'

We were both roughly handled and led away. But I felt such love for these people and prayed that the Lord would reveal himself to them. Respectable people in Nanxun asked us to try again. Which we did. I climbed up on to the stage in my Chinese attire and William remained in the audience.

I cried out for the people to stop this behaviour and listen to what we had to say. Again I was dragged off the stage. I cried out as I was being manhandled away from the crowd, 'Pity your own souls. What you see around you is wrong. Isn't what I am saying true?'

Just then I heard a man say to me, 'What you say is true. I will buy you a drink of tea.'

He purchased both of us some tea and very shortly a crowd of men gathered round. They were curious to hear why we had disrupted the play and what it was that we wanted to tell them. The questions came quick and fast.

'Are all our gods and idols false?'

'If Jesus is in heaven how can we worship him here?'

'Take me to see God and Jesus,' asked one, 'and then I will believe.'

I discussed their questions for hours on end.

Patiently I asked them, 'Your idols have eyes but do they see? They have ears but do they hear you when you pray? They have mouths but do they speak? Can they preserve you from robbers, from quarrels, from sickness or disaster? Have your idols helped you in any way whatsoever?' They all shook their heads. Yet, I could tell them of countless ways, amazing ways, in which God had helped me.

One man asked 'What is good about believing in Jesus?' I told him about freedom from guilt, from sin, from judgement. I told him about a God who loved him and wanted to be his Lord and his friend. I told him about a God who loved him so much that he sent his only son, Jesus Christ, to die instead of him.

As the tea boy went about filling our cups someone asked him, 'Do you believe this God then?'

'Yes I do,' he whispered quietly.

Another man came to me and said, 'I too am far away from home. My family is far away in another part of China. I too am alone without friends and among a people who speak a strange language. Do you feel lonely or does God your father prevent it?'

I smiled. Amelia you know the problems I have had.

I replied to my new friend, 'There are times when I do feel lonely. Particularly when I feel unwell. Often I long for my dear parents and relations. But then I kneel down and pray for them and God puts a little heaven into my heart. Although the desire for home is not removed, I am enabled to wait until I meet them again, wherever and whenever that may be.'

It is so good, Amelia, to know that one more person has heard about the goodness of God.

Amelia sighed. You could laugh about Hudson needing a wife when he was telling you about dressing up as a China man, shaving his head and growing a pigtail, but when it came down to the fact that he was so lonely, it wasn't a laughing matter. She wondered if he had received her letter about Benjamin yet? The engagement wasn't finalised but it wouldn't be long.

Hudson's letters sometimes hinted at his poverty. Other times they were more blatant. The CES had sent him no money for six months. Apparently they had heard that some people were sending Hudson personal gifts so thought that they need not be so conscientious about their own wages to him. Amelia didn't know what to do. That was why she had come out into the fresh air. Sitting, on her own, in a quiet field she felt closer to God. Undisturbed she prayed for her brother, alone in China and for her new life with Benjamin. 'Please, Lord, I am so happy. Can Hudson be happy too?'

***

Mrs Taylor prayed about Hudson's loneliness too and the difficulties he faced. She prayed over his letters. She was anxious at the news some of them brought.

I returned from Shantou today to find that fire had destroyed the warehouse and all its contents. Thirty thousand New Testaments and all my medical supplies and equipment went up in smoke. A letter also arrived just as I was sorting through the awful mess. It appears that Elizabeth has quite made up her mind. She will not marry me. The decision has been made.

Amelia and Mrs Taylor both continually brought Hudson to the Lord in prayer. They rejoiced at prayers answered and wept as they read the pain and heartache in some of his letters.

However, over the months the references to a Maria Dyer became more and more frequent. Amelia wondered at this girl that her brother repeatedly mentioned. Hudson still insisted on wearing his pigtail and Chinese clothes yet it seemed as though this girl could see past the clothes to the man. As well as that, it seemed as though, she respected him for the decision he had taken. Amelia and Louisa both were very curious about the whole situation.

The months prior to Hudson's sudden interest in Maria Dyer had been months of intense depression. He had even toyed with the idea of giving up on China altogether. Many of the missionaries in Shanghai still resented Hudson's clothing. They thought it 'unseemly', 'disgraceful' and 'very bad taste.' He was very down-hearted and discouraged. Before his heart was touched by Maria he still felt as though he loved Elizabeth. If he went back to England her father would let him marry her. And when his fellow missionaries didn't respect him, what was the use of carrying on. Maria Dyer had other opinions.

Hudson Taylor impressed her from the very first time she met him. He too longed after holiness, usefulness and nearness to God. Hudson was different to everybody else she had ever met. He made her feel at rest and understood. He lived in a real world with such a real and great God. She saw little of him but felt comforted when he was near. She felt startled to find how much she missed him when he was away.

Hudson's interest was sparked in the young Miss Dyer as he saw her own missionary zeal and love for the lost people of China. In a letter home he mentioned Miss Dyer as being,

spiritually minded and a true missionary.

Words like this made Amelia and Mrs Taylor sit up and take notice. Gone were the references to Elizabeth and the tortured, anguished heartache. Instead Hudson talked about a warm and steady friendship growing between two young people. The friendship and subsequent romance was altogether healthier than anything he had experienced before, but it was still as passionate. Hudson knew no other way to love than to love with all his heart. Maria Dyer was cut from the same cloth.

However, the path of true love never runs smooth. In one letter Hudson confided to his family the problems he was facing.

Miss Dyer is a truly wonderful person. I have written her a letter, which took some courage as I do not know how she feels for me. I asked her if she would allow me to get to know her with a view to marriage. I begged her not to send me a hasty refusal. Ridicule of that sort would be far too painful for me. I ended with a request that she burn the letter if she found it unacceptable.

Maria apparently was overjoyed and immediately told her sister, Burella, who was overjoyed to hear her sister's good news. Often Maria had confided in her sister about her feelings for this unique young missionary. Maria then ran downstairs to share the good news with her friend and guardian Miss Aldersey who immediately retorted, 'I suppose you will not think of accepting him. Mr Taylor is a young, poor, unconnected nobody. How dare he presume to think of such a thing? Of course the proposal must be refused at once!'

Maria was distraught. She and her sister worked in the Ningbo school under Miss Aldersey. Maria, though under no obligation to do as Miss Aldersey said, respected the wishes of the lady she loved. Miss Aldersey had done a lot for both her and her sister. Other friends also urged obedience and as a result Maria wrote Hudson a letter of refusal. However, she desperately prayed that Hudson would read between the lines. In her own heart she wanted to encourage him. She just hoped that he would be wise enough to see behind the letter to the love in her heart.

Maria sent the letter, which had been passed by Miss Aldersey for approval. All she could do was wait and trust in God. Hudson read it and realised it could be read in two ways. Amelia remained interested too as letters filtered through explaining her brother's blossoming love for Maria. As her own engagement progressed and marriage plans were made for the future, Hudson Taylor's plans moved on too.

I have left the CES. They have failed to send me my quarterly amounts, as promised. I have decided to rely entirely on the Lord for all my needs. He will answer my prayers. I have not given up on Maria either, mother. Hopefully by the time you receive this letter Maria will not be forbidden to me. My friend, Mrs Jones, has told Miss Aldersey herself that she should not tamper with the affections of two young people. I have decided to take matters into my own hands and will speak to Miss Aldersey myself.

Amelia prayed for him. His letters were never frequent enough but news eventually filtered through that he was desperately in love. However things weren't going his way.

My meeting with Miss Aldersey did not go well. I have now written Maria's guardians. Before I did this I asked Maria's friend if Maria loved me in the way that I loved her.

Her friend hesitated before replying, 'Yes, Hudson, she loves you.' My heart sings!

Louisa rejoiced to hear the latest romantic news from China. It seemed as though romance was everywhere these days. Amelia and Benjamin planned their wedding day together and their new home in Bayswater. They also wondered about the possibility of working for the Lord in China. Often Amelia would discuss Hudson's situation with her mother.

'He loves her, Mother, that is certain.'

'Yes, Amelia, Hudson has a great heart. We have seen it given away before.'

'But this time it is different, I'm sure. She is in China. She sounds as dedicated and loving as Hudson. I can hardly believe that there is another person in the world as committed as he is to China - yet Maria Dyer appears to be just that.'

'I hope you are right.'

Then one day Amelia sat down with her journal in her hand and wrote.

The letter we have been expecting came today. Hudson has married Maria. At last it has happened. There have been so many difficulties and barriers but God has brought both of them through it all. Many people have tried to put them off, discourage them, forbid them and fool them into thinking that they did not love each other after all. But as soon as Hudson and Maria got past these people and realised the love that they had for each other they both knew there was no other person for them.

Hudson and Maria both decided that they would get engaged regardless of whether Maria's guardians approved or not. In his letters he tells us of such a strong bond between them even distance cannot truly separate them. Hudson rushed to the bedside of a fellow missionary who was dying from smallpox. The fever claimed the missionary's life and almost killed Hudson too. A couple of days afterwards Hudson also lay sick and feverish and on the point of death. When Hudson woke from a fever he saw Maria standing there, serene and loving and urging him back to recovery. Hudson marvels about her in his letter.

'She came in noiselessly as a breath of air and I felt such a tranquillity steal over me - I knew she must be there. I felt spellbound for a short time, but at length without opening my eyes I put out my hand and she took it so tenderly and with such a soft warm grasp that I could not refrain from a look of gratitude. She motioned me not to speak and put her other hand on my forehead. I felt the headache and the fever retire before her soft hand. 'Don't be afraid or uneasy,' she said 'I am your Maria, and you my dear Hudson. Keep tranquil and try to sleep.'

And he did. It is strange to think of Hudson loving someone more than me, sharing things with someone else that he will not share with me any more. He has someone closer now. And I do too or, at least, I will shortly. The wedding is not that far away for me now.

I laugh though as I remember that letter he sent me some time back, I quote: 'I was not long engaged without trying to make up for the number of sweet kisses I ought to have had over the last few months.'

January 20, 1858, was the marriage day. It was beautiful and the sun shone brightly. Both Hudson and Maria have written to me to tell me about their lovely day. They are so sweet and so in love! Maria is just twenty-one years old and wrote the following letter:

'Dear Amelia,

Hudson and I are now man and wife and I now have a whole new family. You my newest sister, I am longing to meet. Our wedding day was beautiful. The sun shone brightly. I wore a grey silk dress and Hudson wore a Chinese gown. He still wears his pigtail. I wondered at first whether I should ask him to change that and he was willing for my sake to do so but I have since changed my mind. Hudson is Hudson. I fell in love with this man and his pigtail and have no wish to change him.

The only sorrow at our wedding was the absence of my friend, Miss Aldersey, who still insists that I am committing a foolish and selfish act by marrying my darling Hudson.

Our celebrations after the wedding were finer than we could ever have hoped for. The American consul gave us the use of his Sedan Chair. That is quite an honour. It is a method of transport which is used by the more well off members of Chinese society. Hudson and I climbed in and two Chinese men carried the chair which is supported by a set of poles at each end. Twenty-four of our friends met with us including some officers from the British navy who had just arrived in the harbour.

We leave in the next couple of days for the monastery. It is situated up in the mountains above Ningbo. We both long to escape the heat of summer and to start our married life together. Hudson now wishes to write, so I will say goodbye dearest sister, and wish you every blessing in God's name.

Love, Maria

Dear Amelia,

Maria is as sweet as she sounds. We are so happy! God has answered all our prayers; overruled the opposition of those who would have separated us; we can trust in him. We will write you once the honeymoon is over. We both wish you well for your own marriage, Amelia. Till we meet again.

Yours Hudson.'

Amelia placed the journal back in the pocket of her coat. She sighed. Many days had moments like this - moments when it hit you that your brother was living his life at the other side of the world.

'Till we meet again, he says. When will that be?'

Tears blurred her vision as she wandered home.

***

At first Hudson and Maria enjoyed life. But heartache was never far from their door. Maria's sister, Burella, died from cholera at twenty-three years of age. Hudson and Maria's first child was also born two months premature and died. But the love of God strengthened them.

Again and again we dedicated our baby to the Lord God and surely he accepted the intentions of our heart.

Then on a glorious Sunday morning, July 31, 1859, Grace Dyer Taylor was born into the world. Hudson wrote home, 'I have longed for a little miniature of my precious Maria and here she is lying in my arms.' Little Grace brought joy to Hudson and Maria's lives. She made their family complete.

The news eventually filtered home over the oceans and another mother rejoiced at the news of her first grandchild. Amelia and Louisa relished the thought of being Aunt Amelia and Aunt Louisa.

However, as it happened, Hudson had to be separated from his young family. It was an anxious time for them all. Intense heat in the Province had brought on rioting against the foreigners. Maria was persuaded to leave for the safety of a nearby hospital compound. Maria wrote to Hudson on her arrival at the hospital.

My own precious love, Dr and Mrs Parker have kindly received your fugitive wife. When shall I kiss you again and feel your loving arms around me? God bless you my own precious Hudson, my husband, keep you from all harm.

These intense emotions may seem strange if you have not lived through the circumstances that Hudson and Maria lived through. However out of two hundred men who entered China as missionaries, since 1807, over forty had lost their lives. The wives of fifty-one of these two hundred men also perished. Working for God in China was a dangerous life and Hudson and Maria knew it.

More responsibilities were eventually placed on Hudson as a result of Dr Parker leaving the hospital after the death of his wife. Hudson took over where Parker had left off and the strain began to tell.

Maria worried constantly about his haggard complexion and decreasing weight. The situation got worse and worse. The hospital was in desperate need of financial assistance. One morning the cook came in to announce that they had opened the last bag of rice.

Hudson, slowly looked up and said, 'Then the Lord's time must surely be near to meet our need.'

Sure enough a letter arrived. A friend had inherited a legacy and had decided to write to the Taylors.

I shall not be altering my standard of living. The enclosed fifty pounds is to be used at your discretion. Will you kindly indicate how much more can be used?

Hudson and Maria translated the letter to all their assistants and 'Hallelujahs' sounded from every corner of the hospital. The Chinese assistants rushed into all the wards with the good news. They had been saved, as it were, by the skin of their teeth. God's timing was perfect. But a few months later a letter arrived at Barnsley. Mrs Taylor prayed over it not knowing whether to weep tears of anxiety or cry with joy.

It appears that my work exceeds my time and my strength. I should inform you that for some time my health has been failing. I have felt more and more unequal to my work. It is very difficult to be your own physician. I think, however that my chest is affected with tubercular disease. My liver and spleen are also infected. It may be that I shall be sent home for a season.

An independent medical opinion was sought and it was decreed that it was high time that Hudson left China. June 1860 arrived and Hudson and Maria decided it was time to leave, perhaps for good. 'Who knows if we shall see China again?' thought Maria as they prepared to bid farewell to the land they had grown to love and care for. The emotions at Barnsley in Yorkshire were quite different when they heard of Hudson and Maria's plans to return.

'Hudson's coming home! Thank you God, thank you!'

A Vision begins

Louisa and Amelia ran down the lane, their aprons flapping in the wind, wisps of hair escaping from their well secured hair pins. They were both a lot older now. Hudson had left in 1853 and it was now 1860 - only seven years but it was amazing what changes seven years could bring. Amelia was finally getting the last few things completed before her wedding in a couple of month's time. The only thing to draw a shadow on the plans was the fact that Hudson would miss the wedding by a matter of months. But there was nothing that could be done about it. Both Amelia and Benjamin had waited to get married for long enough and they were anxious to open a new chapter in their lives.

Louisa and Amelia walked past the church yard and on into the cool of the dense, green woodland. Louisa was smiling. Amelia stood straining her neck to look at the flecks of blue that broke through the dark greens and emeralds of the leaves above. A breeze blew through them and the sound reminded Amelia of thousands of voices whispering at her, peacefully, excitedly. Everything was going to be fine now. Hudson was coming home. The letter had arrived that morning. The excitement had been so frantic that Amelia and Louisa had just had to get out of the kitchen and run the emotion out of their systems.

The odd curtain had twitched, as the two Taylor girls made a scene running wildly down the road, aprons flapping in the breeze. Now everything was calm except for their deep breathing as they came to rest at the foot of a giant oak.

Louisa looked sideways at her sister who was still gazing at the flickering leaves and listening avidly to the cascading sound. She ran her hand down the gnarled old roots of the oak tree.

Amelia smiled and slipped her arm round her sister's waist - it was a perfect day. What made it even more perfect for her and for the whole Taylor family was that it was the first day that the whole family had shared as believers in the Lord. Louisa had just told them with tears in her eyes and excitement in her voice that she had become a Christian. Sitting together under the old oak tree the two sisters felt closer than they had ever felt before. They both lay back against the strong, spreading oak, its branches waving far above them. A gentle breeze blew through the woods.

'The first day of spring,' Amelia whispered as they continued to gaze heavenward.

**

Thankfully there was enough time for Louisa to dash off a letter to Hudson. It arrived just before Hudson and Maria left to join their ship. Hudson replied in the midst of hurried preparations for the trip down the Yangtze river into the China Sea.

'It's amazing,' he said to Maria as she packed another chest to be taken back to England. 'Louisa has always been an independent creature. All the family have been pressuring her to make a decision and it's taken her twenty years to finally make up her mind. But now that she's made it there will be no stopping her. I've written her a letter. If we post it today it may arrive before us.'

Maria picked up the letter and read.

Cleave to the Lord, my dear sister (now doubly my sister) with true purpose of heart and you will find your joy to be full.

On July 18, 1860, Hudson, Maria and baby Grace set off on what was to be a four month voyage. Despite dysentery, bed bugs and an obnoxious captain who objected to little Grace's crying they arrived in the United Kingdom, safe and sound.

They brought with them a Chinese helper who they had persuaded to come with them to the United Kingdom. Hudson, Maria, Grace and their Chinese friend all trundled onto a train which took them to Bayswater in London. Amelia's wedding had taken place and this was now her home. What a reunion it was!

'HUDSON!'

Even before he had alighted from the cab he heard Amelia's voice. Before he knew where he was there were two young women flinging themselves at him. Louisa was there too. Both girls were so excited that they neglected to notice that Hudson was still wearing his Chinese clothes and that the pigtail still occupied a prominent position on his head. Hudson was home at last and nothing else mattered.

Maria sat watching the goings on, smiling warmly. These were two women she had heard so much about and felt she knew intimately through letters and Hudson's memories. Grace gurgled in amusement at the scene before her. Soon Hudson was forgotten and Amelia and Louisa became two doting aunts.

Throughout the preceding weeks Louisa made it her personal mission to update Maria on all the latest fashions. Both Amelia and Louisa tried to persuade Hudson that his Chinese costume was no longer necessary. Eventually he agreed. So when the time came for the family reunion, in Barnsley, Hudson had a smart fashionable suit to wear and Maria looked stunning in a silk crinoline skirt and jacket to match.

When the door to the little chemist's in Barnsley was finally opened to receive again the young man, who had left several years previously, there wasn't a dry eye in the house except for little Grace. She was nice and snug in the arms of her grandmother, who held her and rocked her back and fore praying prayers of love and protection over her head. This was a day Mrs Amelia Taylor had wondered if she would ever see.

There were soon other children to be held and prayed over. That April saw the birth of Hudson and Maria's first son, Herbert Hudson. The following months and years saw Hudson becoming a fully qualified member of the Royal College of Surgeons. He even spent many hours updating a Chinese New Testament. However, his doctor had told him emphatically that a return to China was not possible for several years. In November 1862 Hudson also passed his midwifery examinations so Maria had a well-qualified attendant when their second son, Frederick, was born on the 23rd of November, that same year.

Another year was spent hearing news from China and longing to be back where they could carry on their work and help their friends and colleagues who were still there. Meanwhile Hudson and Maria made friends with many other Christians including Charles Spurgeon and George Müller. Then, on June 24, 1864, a third son, Samuel, was born. The house the Taylors were living in was far too small for four young children and their parents so they moved, in the October of that year, to a much bigger place.

However, Hudson was on the brink of a decision which would change his life. In 1865 he wrote a small book entitled *China: Its Spiritual Need and Claims*. He brought to the reader's attention China's immense size:

> If all the Chinese were to march past at the rate of thirty miles a day, they would move on, day after day, week after week, month after month and over seventeen and a quarter years would elapse before the last one passed by. Can Christians sit with folded arms while these multitudes perish - perish for lack of knowledge - for lack of that knowledge which we possess so richly?
>
> What does the master teach us? Is it not that if one sheep out of a hundred be lost, we are to leave the ninety and nine and seek that one? But here the proportions are almost reversed, and we stay at home with the one sheep and take no heed to the ninety and nine perishing ones! Christian think of the command of our great Captain and Leader 'Go ye into all the world and preach the gospel to every creature.' Think of the millions upon millions in poor China to whom no one has brought the good news of salvation.

Hudson knew that something had to happen. He knew that something had to replace the CES but what?

He calculated that there were eleven provinces that did not have any missionary contact. These eleven provinces needed at least twenty-two missionaries if they were going to be reached with the gospel. But could God supply them or was this plan far too ambitious, Hudson pondered.

All this time Hudson believed that a million a month were dying without Christ in China. The pressure of this conviction was almost too much and the stress of Hudson's worries and concerns for China began to show. It was decided that he needed a break So, Hudson Taylor was packed off to Brighton for a weekend's rest and relaxation.

The church he went to wasn't that great. He didn't feel as if he belonged. He soon left the building to walk, alone, on the Brighton sands. He had been

Unable to bear the sight of a congregation of a thousand or more Christian people rejoicing in their own security, while millions were perishing for lack of knowledge

There, in deep spiritual agony, the Lord conquered Hudson's unbelief and he surrendered himself to God once more.

I told him that all the responsibility as to the issues and consequences must rest with him; that as his servant I would obey and follow him. It was his responsibility to direct, care for, and to guide me and those who might labour with me.

Peace at once flowed into Hudson's burdened heart and immediately he asked God for twenty-four fellow workers, two for each of the eleven inland provinces which were without a missionary, and two for Mongolia. As the surf pounded on the Brighton sands Hudson took out his

Bible and wrote his prayer in the margin. He would have a record of this moment to look back on during the coming years. Hudson had a record of the fact that he had prayed to God for help. When God provided this help Hudson would look back on this brief scrawl and smile.

He returned home refreshed. Hudson had a peace - he knew that God would bless this work.

At the very first opportunity Hudson went to the London and County Bank and opened an account under the name 'China Inland Mission'. The opening amount was £10, not much, but as Hudson said some time later, 'It was £10 and all the promises of God.'

When Hudson set up the CIM he also set up some rules that had to be kept. Hudson and Maria would be in charge of the new recruits as they were the only ones with any experience of China. In exchange Hudson would provide the new recruits with the basic training and equipment they needed for life in China.

Missionaries were not to be drawn out of any particular denomination, but from all the leading Christian churches, provided they could sign a simple doctrinal declaration.

The missionaries were not guaranteed a salary but were to trust in the Lord to supply their needs. Income would be shared. No debts were to be incurred.

No appeals for funds would be made.

Work abroad would be directed not by committees at home but by Hudson Taylor himself and other leaders on the spot in China. The activities of the mission must be systematic and practical. A comprehensive plan to evangelise the whole of China was to be set up.

As a courtesy to the Chinese all CIM personnel would wear Chinese clothes and worship in buildings built in the Chinese style.

May 26, 1866, saw Hudson Taylor and Maria and their small family of four set sail again for China aboard *The Lammermuir*. Only, this time, they took with them a team of sixteen missionaries and the China Inland Mission began.

As the boat sailed across the oceans, bringing the Taylors back to China once again, many crew members came to know the Lord - and others too. Little Grace not even eight years old at the time, simply put her trust in the Lord Jesus Christ. The prayers that had been prayed over her, by her grandmother, when she first set her eyes on her first grandchild, were answered. It didn't matter what awaited them on Chinese soil Grace was safe and sound in the hands of her loving creator. Hudson and Maria breathed a sigh of relief for that. They knew the coming months would be hard. They just didn't know how hard.

Troubles begin

The fledgling CIM had troubles of its own. Bickering amongst the missionaries and bad feeling dogged its early days. In fact, the situation became so dangerous, the mission was in danger of collapse even before it had begun. But one dreadful and tragic event soon changed all that.

It started on an August day, on a hilltop holiday where the Taylors had gone to escape the great heat. Grace went off her food and began to lose weight rapidly. She complained of a headache and then a high fever set in.

The letter said:

The diagnosis was meningitis.

Mrs Taylor sat in the rocking chair, rocking back and fore, holding the faded letter in her wrinkled hands. She remembered that morning, not that long ago, when she had held in her arms a delightfully chubby little child and had marvelled that she had ever lived to see that day. Children dying was a tragic, but all too frequent, event in England and in China too. Mrs Taylor, however, had never thought that when she said goodbye to Grace - it would be for the last time. Mrs Taylor pictured little Grace lying ill and in severe pain and she cried bitterly. The fever had attacked the young child making her incoherent and sapping the life from out of her. As Mrs Taylor read on she saw her young son go to the side of the bed where his young daughter lay and whisper in her ear, 'I think Jesus is going to take you to himself. You are not afraid to trust yourself with him, are you?'

She rejoiced at her little grandchild's reply.

'No Papa,' she whispered.

Hudson had known the risks of taking his family to the inhospitable climate of the Far East. But he had trusted God to take care of them. Hudson knew how well his God had taken care of them. He knew that his little girl was safe for ever and for this he was thankful.

The end came all too soon. Pneumonia set in and Grace lost consciousness. Hudson remained at her bedside and sang hymns as Grace lingered. Maria sat, hunched over her little daughter, unwilling to leave her even for a moment. August 23rd, at twenty minutes to nine, Grace's breathing stopped.

The letter was very difficult to read. It was even harder to tell Amelia and Louisa what had happened. Hudson cried by himself for several days and wondered, 'Is it possible that I shall never feel the pressure of that little hand, never hear the sweet prattle of those dear lips, nor see the sparkle of those bright eyes? And yet she is not lost. I would not have her back again.'

In the midst of heartache the work of the CIM went on. The missionaries moved away from the coast to areas where Westerners were hardly known. In fact it is believed that the death of young Grace actually brought greater unity to the fledgling missionary organisation. Perhaps this tragedy even stopped the petty bickering and squabbles that had been rife since the arrival of the new and inexperienced, missionaries.

However, the increased activities of the CIM caused opposition amongst some of the population. The gospel's emphasis on the individual was against the Chinese ethic that family was more important than the individual. The missionaries' message, it was feared, would undermine the fabric of traditional society. Wild accusations were made about the missionaries. People hurled insults at them in the streets. The missionaries continued with their work though they were fearful sometimes for their lives. It must have been difficult to bring up a family in that atmosphere. Hudson and Maria would certainly have felt anxious, particularly as they had recently received another little life into the world. She was named Maria, after her mother.

The local situation, however, came to a head one evening, almost a year after Grace's death. Hudson had to station guards at the entrance to the mission compound as the crowd outside the mission gates was in a very ugly mood. On August the 22nd the crowd had grown to a gigantic number of about 10,000. Some were armed with knives, spears and clubs. The situation was desperate and verging on anarchy. The Yangzhou riots began.

'The Foreign Devils have eaten twenty-four children' the cry went up. The accusation was absolutely ridiculous but nobody thought to investigate the rumour. The crowd just lapped up the scandal and hysteria resulted.

Hudson had to get help as the crowd was whipped up to higher levels of frenzy. He prayed for his family before getting out by the back of the compound. Eventually, however, Hudson had to get onto the main street and he and a friend were pounded with stones and bricks. They finally made it to the local mandarin's quarters where they shouted with all their might, 'Save life! Save life!' a cry that no mandarin can ignore. The mandarin was finally persuaded that no harm had come to any children. The crowd was quieted and the two men escorted home safely.

However, on arrival they found a pile of burnt reeds outside the house. They realised that there had been an attempt to burn the place. The report was that all the foreigners, left behind in the house, had been killed. Hudson was sickened and horrified and prayed desperately that this report was at least exaggerated. But as they searched the premises there was no sign of Maria or any of the families. The report they had received must have been true!

***

Amelia, however, wrote the exciting truth to her mother one day.

It turns out that Maria and the children were, in actual fact, quite safe, despite the ordeal they had just lived through. Maria was upstairs with them, Freddie, Bertie, Samuel and the little baby Maria. As she sat there nursing Bertie, who was by that stage almost beside himself with hysteria, a voice called out from below the window.

'Mrs Taylor. They're setting the house on fire. Get out if you can for we can't help you.'

Maria opened the window and looked below. She then realised, mother, that the only avenue of escape which was available to them was through the window. Maria and others in the room with her began to throw mattresses and bed linen out the window to soften any falls.

'Quick pass the children down,' a dry and rasping voice was heard to say from just beneath the window. One of the men had managed to climb on to the sloping roof that reached to just below the bedroom window. Someone grabbed Freddie, and was about to lower him down, when Maria gasped, 'No take Bertie first. He's so frightened.' So Bertie went first, closely, followed by Freddie. The children were quickly ushered away from the house by two other missionaries just in the nick of time. A bare-chested man barged his way into the bedroom. Maria saw another man, with a bundle of clothing, running down the stairs. Another woman pulled a chest roughly out of a nearby room. But Maria didn't care about that. There were far more important things to worry about - mainly the lives of her children and the friends and colleagues with her in the bedroom.

'We are all women and children here' she shouted at the intruder. 'Aren't you ashamed to molest us?'

The man took no notice of her arguments and proceeded to do a body search of all the woman and children present. It was humiliating, but to struggle might have endangered their lives, so they let him continue. One of the young women had hidden a bag of coins, under her dress, which was roughly taken from her, another had a clasp in her hair, which they tore off. Maria's wedding ring was also taken. Thankfully one of the women had the sense to pick up baby Maria and make a run for it down the stairs. I suppose in all the chaos and noise no one noticed one woman and a baby. Her name was Annie, and she ran through the flames to safety, where the others were waiting.

Meanwhile a rope of sheets was hung out the window. The others were winched down to safety. Now only Maria and two other women were left. However, the mob set fire to a heap of wood, and left it under the window, making it virtually impossible for Maria and the others to make their escape via that route. The mob were determined to destroy them.

The noise was incredible as walls all around the house collapsed with the heat. The bare-chested man grabbed Mr Rutland he climbed through the window and dragged him back out onto the roof by his hair. Mr Rutland took off his watch, which was what the intruder was after, and threw it into the darkness. He hoped the intruder would run off and search for it. Instead the man became even angrier and grabbed a brick. He aimed to crush Mr Rutland's skull. However, Maria intervened, at risk to her own life and to the life of her unborn child. (Yes mother, Maria is pregnant again, in the midst of all that horror.)

The intruder was distracted as he called to the other rioters to come up and help him. In that short space of time Maria jumped out the window quickly followed by the others. She landed awkwardly and fractured her elbow. She ran to safety and was overjoyed to see her wide-eyed little children, frightened but alive. Soon soldiers drove off the mob.

Hudson believed that they had all been killed. However, as Maria and the others removed themselves from hiding that rumour was quashed. God had looked after them and Hudson's little family was safe and back together once again.

The mission house is a wreck. Even Maria's Bible was torn to shreds. However, as they gathered the pages together again, they discovered that not one single page was missing. Now I think that is definitely worth noting down.

Mrs Taylor sucked her teeth nervously throughout the whole letter. 'What of the unborn baby? It must have been born by now but I may not hear of it for some weeks yet.'

***

On November 29, 1868, Charles Edward was born into the Taylor family. The years of 1868 and 1869 were going to be difficult years for the Taylor family. Young Samuel suffered almost continuously from tuberculosis enteritis. Mrs Taylor wrote about Hudson and Maria's difficult situation to Amelia, sharing her anxiety about her young grandson.

Maria and Hudson take him with them everywhere, and the others are left with their nurse, while Hudson and Maria continue with their travels. This is not working out that well, however, as the children left behind are feeling very unsettled and upset. As a result they are all quite prone to falling sick. I am not sure what Hudson and Maria shall do. They will have to think and pray a lot about it as it is a situation that surely cannot continue.

Amelia held the letter from her mother in one hand and another letter she had just received from an agonised Maria in the other.

...but Amelia, Hudson and I have come to a decision. We have prayed a lot. The situation healthwise for the children has become so difficult we have decided to send them back to Britain. Herbert and Freddie, Samuel and Maria will leave China with their nurse, Emily Blatchley. We are especially worried about Samuel. He will not survive another summer here...

Amelia didn't envy their decision.

***

The weeks before the children's departure passed by in a flurry of packing. Samuel's health, however, deteriorated rapidly. Tragically, as the little family prepared to leave the city for the port, he showed signs of relapse. The little boy, only five years old, didn't even make it to the boat and was buried in the cemetery at Chinkiang.

Now two of Maria's little ones were safe in heaven. The love of their Lord and Saviour, Jesus Christ, was the only thing that kept the parents going as they waved goodbye to the other weeping children. Maria, Hudson and baby Charles returned home alone.

***

Months later the young Taylor children were now settling into the strange routine of a life without parents. They stayed with well-off supporters of Hudson and Maria, Mr and Mrs Berger.

Amelia loved Hudson and Maria's children almost as dearly as her own. One day she received a letter from Hudson. Walking to the parlour she tore open the envelope and gasped at the dreadful news. 'How will we tell the children? How awful, to lose your own mother when not even your father can be at your side to comfort you.'

Maria was dead.

An end or a beginning?

Mrs Taylor rocked back and fore on her chair. Maria had caught the same disease that had killed Samuel. Maria had suffered from a high fever. Her pregnancy did not go well and the young baby died at only thirteen days old. From then on things got worse - internal bleeding and the severe summer heat left Maria weak. The one relief for the young mother, only thirty-three years old, was that the children had arrived safe and well in the United Kingdom. The little baby, Noel, was buried alongside his brother Samuel not far from the river at Zhenjiang.

Maria had been too weak to attend the funeral. Mrs Taylor wept as she read Hudson's letter.

She placed a thin arm on my arm and kissed me then she dozed off to sleep. At 2 a.m. I gave her some more food and medicine and sat with her until three. As the sun rose I could see that Maria was dying.

'My darling,' I said, 'Do you know that you are dying?'

'Dying!' she said. 'What makes you think so?'

'I can see it darling. Your strength is giving way.'

'Can it be so? I feel no pain, only weariness?'

'Yes, you are going home. You will soon be with Jesus.'

'I am so sorry dear,' she sighed.

'You are not sorry to go to be with Jesus ?'

'Oh no, it's not that. You know darling, there hasn't been a cloud between my soul and the Saviour for ten years past. I cannot be sorry to go to him. But I am sorry to leave you alone at this time. Yet he will be with you and meet all your need.'

As she lost strength, and I realised that her time was coming fast, I allowed friends to come and see her one last time. I will always remember her last greeting to those Chinese we knew who had not accepted the Lord as their Saviour.

'Come to Jesus and meet me in heaven.'

Our Chinese servants and friends loved her so much. We all did. She gave me a kiss for Herbert, Freddie and Maria and a message for them all. Then she could speak no more. She fell asleep and, as the night drew on, her sleep became lighter and lighter, until she passed from us. She is now gone.

Hudson knelt by the bed and prayed.

Dear God, thank you for giving my darling Maria to me. Thank you for the twelve and a half years of happiness we have had together. Thank you for taking her to your own blessed presence. I dedicate myself anew to your service. Amen.

***

Soon it was time for Hudson to come home for a short time. He had to see his children. Little Charles was reunited with his brothers and sister. Amelia grew closer to all the Taylor children. She was a much loved aunt and mother figure to them. That year's journal had a few insights into the continuing life of Hudson Taylor. Amelia glanced at an old entry dated a few months after Maria's death.

Is this the end? Will Hudson be everything that he is supposed to be without Maria? Lord God, Hudson has been set apart for you for his life. I am sure that he still has so much more to offer. His life hasn't ended yet.

This was true. The CIM would go from strength to strength. Hudson was with his children again and had also remarried someone who had loved Maria as a dear sister and friend. Hudson married Jennie Faulding another missionary to China and together they continued the work. Amelia picked up her journal and once again began to write.

They now have an ever expanding collection of children - ten in total and I have grown to love them all as much as my own. Tomorrow, the Taylor family leave again for China. The work must continue. The work that Hudson started, that Maria died for and that Hudson and Jennie must continue - to glorify the Lord Jesus Christ in China, to bring him to the lost of that land. There are still so many people who haven't heard about Christ. There is still so much work to do. Hudson has done so much for you Lord. Yet it is nothing compared to what you have done for us by forgiving our sins and dying on the cross. In fact Hudson looks on it as a privilege to work for God, to bring others to the knowledge of salvation. I remember now a story he told me about a young man. What was his name? Ah! His name was Ni.

It was a hot day, and Hudson had been sitting in the shade, beneath a cherry tree, sipping some hot tea. It was market day and the town was busy. Some people came to sit next to him. Conversations occurred naturally. People were anxious to hear truth.

A young Chinese man, named Ni joined the cluster of people surrounding Hudson. However, Ni noted that this missionary was different - the long flowing robes and jet black pig-tail made him more approachable somehow and less threatening. Ni was tired of living a life that gave no hope or peace of heart. He listened avidly to what was being discussed over the steaming tea.

'You say that all I have to do is to ask for forgiveness and that your God will give it to me without charge? All because of his Son Jesus Christ?' he said astonished.

'Yes! Jesus died instead of us. It is because of what he did that we can have forgiveness and a new life.'

Ni was amazed. 'I have been waiting for truth like this all my life.' He then looked puzzled and added, 'How long has your country known about this truth? How long have you known about Jesus Christ?'

Hudson could hardly bring himself to tell the man the shameful news 'We have know about the Lord Jesus Christ for several hundred years.'

Ni gasped, 'And you have only come to tell us about it now. My father searched for truth but never found it. You came in time for me but you came too late for him. He died last month...' Ni sighed and then did what everyone should do when they hear really good news. He told people. He shouted out in the middle of the market place, 'From now on I believe in Jesus!'

Hudson thanked God that another person had come to Christ. He walked slowly back up the road, away from the sights and sounds of the Shanghai market place.

Each day seems to be an adventure with God for my brother. Each day begins with the dark orange sun rising above the teeming city and each day sees new lives come into the world. However, as the sun rises Hudson sees another side to the teaming city. He sees the thousands who die each day without the knowledge of Jesus Christ. Hudson cannot sit and do nothing while people perish. Nor should I.

With that Amelia laid her journal to one side. She had her own part to play in this great missionary adventure. Bowing her head, she prayed.

***

Some say that Hudson Taylor's adventure ended on June the 3rd 1905 when this pioneer missionary finally breathed his last. Of course some say that was when his adventure really began. But one thing is certain, Hudson

Taylor's legacy continues. God called Hudson Taylor to China. Today he still calls people to work for him in countries all round the world. Are you ready for an adventure?

A New Adventure

The distracting drumbeat of traffic threatened to disturb Lauren's concentration as she began to pen her weekly letter home. That and the heat. Early summer in China was like living in an oven permanently set at gas mark seven. Her hand was moist and stuck to the flimsy, white, writing paper. The plastic biro slipped between her fingers and smeared a blue ink smudge under 'Dad'.

'Dear Mum and Dad ... smudge,' Lauren sighed. 'Bother, hardly an achievement for five minutes' worth of effort.'

She put down her pen, pushed back her red plastic chair and trudged over to the doorway. She clicked the fan up a notch and watched as the rusting blades rotated themselves into a frenzy, thrashing at the still air. The breeze on Lauren's face refreshed her. The letter slipped to the edge of the table and tumbled end over end on to the bottle green carpet.

'I will write home. Nothing will stand in my way,' Lauren chided herself. Sunday afternoon had always been the time to write her letter to her family in Northern Ireland. It would be at least two weeks before her mother, father and brother would see it, but that was the snail mail Chinese postal service for you.

'Dear Mum, Dad and David, I guess the heat is

getting to me. It's taken ten minutes to get this far. It is *soooo* hot. And the humidity really slows me down. Somehow over the winter I seem to have forgotten what it feels like — dripping with sweat and needing a shower every two hours. You should see me in the classroom. Definitely more perspiration than inspiration! My students don't appear affected at all. I suppose they've always lived with it. Isn't it strange to think this time last year I was getting nervous about boarding the plane to Ganzhou? Now it feels like home...'

It did feel like home. But it had done since the moment she had walked into the flat. Last September, nine months before, the man from the university Foreign Affairs Office had proudly showed 'the new English teacher from Britain' where she would live. As soon as he had left her, she had thrown open her suitcases and begun pinning posters on the yucky white walls. Her nice writing paper had been laid neatly on the desk. Too bad it had long since been used up. This flimsy Chinese paper wasn't attractive at all. Finally she had found the wrapper from a bar of chocolate in her pocket and stuck it on the bedroom door.

Lauren chuckled. 'If the chocolate factory could see my room now, they'd use it in their adverts'. The doors were plastered from top to toe in chocolate bar wrappers.

Crash! Lauren jumped. 'Mr Song! What happened? Are you alright?' Mr Song was the local handyman on the university campus and not an infrequent visitor to her flat. It was rare for a month to go by without some problem needing Mr Song's attention. Today it was the taps on her bath that were leaking badly. The trouble was that Mr Song was a disaster himself. Only last month he had flooded her flat leaving the carpet sodden and the bathroom without water for a week.

'Are you alright, Mr Song?'

The handyman poked his head out of the bathroom and grinned at her with a mouthful of ill-placed teeth. 'Ok.'

Lauren was not convinced. She left her letter and went to find out for herself. Strewn over the bathroom floor tiles were several pieces of plumbing. Water was spraying from both taps like a pair of fountains.

'Mr Song!'

'Ok, ok,' Mr Song repeated.

Although Lauren had learned some Mandarin during her stay in China, the handyman remained sceptical that any Westerner could possibly speak Chinese and only ever replied with 'ok, ok' no matter what Lauren said.

'Mr Song, it is not okay, okay. You'll flood my flat again and have water running down the stairs. Mr Xu from the university office will not be happy.'

'Ok, Ok'. Lauren gestured at the taps.

'Mend them, please. Not demolish them ... okay?'

'Ok, Ok'

'Maybe,' said Lauren and went back to her letter.

Despite his bungling approach to DIY and her feigned annoyance, Mr Song was one of Lauren's favourite Chinese. No matter what happened the skinny, diminutive electrician-cum-plumber-cum joiner seemed to remain unruffled. Strangely, she had discovered, he was an excellent knitter and readily produced sweaters for himself and his family. If only God had blessed him with an ability to mend bathroom taps!

When Mr Song departed fifteen minutes later with a

final cheery 'ok', the bathroom taps were where they should have been, but still dripping. Lauren eyed them critically for several moments and decided the problem was perceptibly worse than before. She was, however, getting on much better with the letter; describing Mr Song's efforts in graphic detail.

'My students are pretty nervous about the end of year exams. After every lesson I have a cluster of anxious individuals running up to my desk. 'Will there be dictation?' (They hate dictation), 'Can you help me with my grammar, Miss Lauren?', 'Can you show me the exam paper?' (Some of their Chinese teachers do — can you believe that? They think if the students do well they must be good teachers. Consequently, hardly anyone ever fails an exam. Some students get really upset if they score less than 90%).'

Lauren pictured herself in front of her oral English class the first morning. All the students had stood politely behind their wooden desks and applauded. Across the blackboard one of them had neatly written 'Welcome our new English teacher Miss Lauren McCallum to Ganzhou Teacher's College'.

To her great consternation all the students looked identical! She wondered quite how she could ever distinguish one from another. Over the next few days she had learned their names. More than once she got her tongue-tied, until some chose English names. Of these 'Stone' stood out as the oddest. No matter how Lauren had tried to convince him that 'Stone' wasn't a proper name, Stone was determined to keep it.

Then she had begun to notice the differences in their

dress. There were most definitely two fashions on show — the country style and the city smarts. The country girls kept their long black hair in ponytails and wore bright, hand made dresses, something the city girls felt very old fashioned. The city boys paraded around in track suits and platform shoes and had their hair permed. To Lauren's amusement they insisted this was the way western men kitted themselves out and produced glossy magazine pages to prove it.

Lauren was also amused by the 'spectacle swapping' that occurred in every class. A quick survey had revealed that virtually all the students needed glasses, but only about a third wore them. Whenever she asked a student to read the blackboard a pair of glasses needed passing back and forth before the task could be undertaken.

The sound of a bicycle sliding to a halt outside made Lauren look up. She glanced through the holes in the mosquito netting which covered the window. Sun Jun Bing! Now Sun Jun Bing was altogether different and easily recognised. At over six feet tall he towered above his classmates, who were generally shorter than Lauren herself. He always wore a suit and tie, even on the hottest days. He had told her he intended to become a businessman and therefore dressed the part. Quite how he had ended up at a teacher training college was still a mystery to Lauren.

Sun Jun Bing was also considerably different in his manner. The other students were conservative, quiet and always took pains to be polite. Not Sun Jun Bing. He was loud and abrasive. In class he asked awkward questions at inappropriate times. Not infrequently did he burp in lessons. 'Oh well, letter. If Sun Jun Bing was here, I can't see you getting much attention' muttered Lauren to herself. A hammering from the door announced that Sun Jun Bing had indeed arrived. 'Who is it?' called Lauren innocently. 'Sun Jun Bing, your student,' came the impatient reply. 'Miss Lauren, can I come in?' Sun Jun Bing bounded in without waiting for a response and disappeared into her living room.

By the time Lauren caught up with him, her student had inspected her letter, examined a pile of papers on the desk, studied a photograph of her parents and was peering through his thick rimmed glasses at her collection of books. 'Have you got a Bible?' Lauren looked at Sun Jun Bing in surprise. 'Yes, of course.' It was no secret amongst her students that she was a Christian. But why did he want to know?

Lauren was well aware that you could not trust every student in college. Some had ambitions to become members of the Chinese Communist Party. Passing on information about the activities of a foreign teacher and her contacts with the students could help their application.

Lauren showed Sun Jun Bing her Bible. Sun Jun Bing nodded excitedly, 'I want a Bible'. 'Why?' Now it was the student's turn to hesitate. 'You won't tell anyone?' Lauren shook her head, wondering what was coming next. 'I listened to radio broadcasts when I was at Middle School. From Hong Kong they said God had written the Bible. At school the teachers tell me God doesn't happen…' 'Exist,' Lauren corrected him. '…God doesn't exist. I thought if God doesn't exist he can't write a book. So I write to Hong Kong to ask for Bible.' He paused and began thumbing through Lauren's library again. 'What happened?' 'Nothing! I wait three years and nothing comes. Maybe they didn't get my letter.' His search along the shelves came to an abrupt end. Sun Jun Bing waved his hand at the last book as though he hoped it would suddenly turn in to a Bible. 'I want a Bible.' Lauren studied him for a moment, still undecided about his motives. 'Alright, wait here.' Satisfied he would not follow her, she went into her bedroom and delved into a plastic bag at the back of her wardrobe. 'This is a New Testament. Not the whole Bible. But it will tell you the stories of Jesus. You remember we talked about Jesus at Christmas and Easter. See it's in Chinese and English.'

Sun Jun Bing grabbed the slim blue paper backed volume from her outstretched hands and flicked through the pages. 'I will read this.' Hurriedly he stuffed the book inside his jacket and strode out to the hallway. 'Don't tell anyone?' 'I won't,' promised Lauren. 'I hope I can find Jesus by the end of it.' 'I hope so too.' Sun Jun Bing sprang down the stairs two at a time, hardly pausing to wave goodbye.

Lauren watched him from her window as he mounted his bicycle and sped away. Who would have thought? Brash, awkward Sun Jun Bing wanted a Bible. He wasn't the first student to come knocking on her door to learn about Jesus, but he was certainly the most unexpected!

She wanted to write home about Sun Jun Bing. But she couldn't. Her letter may be opened and read. She contented herself with a paragraph about the film she had watched with the students, 'Jurassic Park'.

Foreign teachers, western films? It wasn't that long

ago that radio waves were about the only foreign thing that could get over the Chinese border — let alone Irish girls and Hollywood blockbuster movies. Chairman Mao had been on the throne then and it had been a horrid time for the Chinese. He had kicked all the missionaries out of China as well and had closed the churches down.

Lauren knew there had been CIM missionaries in Ganzhou before 1950. An elder in the city church had told her. They had a mission station and ran two schools for boys. There had been a single woman missionary from Britain, Annette, and a family from the states with children Ricky, Dorrie and Pebble. The Chinese boys called Ricky 'Weeky', because they couldn't manage the 'R'.

Annette had been the last CIM-er to leave Ganzhou and head for Hong Kong when the Communists took over. Now, in the nineties, Lauren was the first western Christian to come back to live in the city. Lauren didn't feel nearly as brave and adventurous as the missionaries she had read about in books, but giving Sun Jun Bing a New Testament today was just as important as the work they had done.

'You asked about my plans for the summer. We finish here at the end of June, early July. I want to see more of China. Ganzhou is brilliant, but China is bigger. I plan to take a bus to the provincial capital, Nanchang, then train to Shanghai. Maybe hard sleeper — it's cheaper than soft sleeper and more comfortable than a hard seat. The journey takes the best part of two days. After that I'm not sure. I'll let you know before I leave.

'I have to be back here for the first week in September. All new classes — new students. More names to learn. Some really neat things have happened this term. I can't tell you until I see you. I'm just so sure this is where God wants me to be.

Love to Gramps,
Love Lauren.'

Thinking Further

1   Do you pray? Do you speak to God? Hudson Taylor's parents prayed to God about him even before he was born. Do you know of someone who has prayed for you? Can you think about someone you could pray for? Try and set aside time every day to speak to God. Even if it's just a few minutes to tell God that you love him. Read Psalm 121- Did you know that God never sleeps? God is always listening.

2   What's the hardest thing about growing up? How can knowing God and talking to him help you? Hudson Taylor had a difficult time as a teenager. He felt that people didn't understand him and he hated being told what to do. He wanted to live his own life and make his own choices. Do you ever feel like that? Do you feel that nobody is listening to you? Remember that God is listening and is never too busy. Psalm 4:3; Psalm 94:9. Also remember that we should listen to God. We take a great risk if we ignore God and do not obey his word. Proverbs 19:20 Psalm 81:11-12. Psalm 85:8; John 14:23.

3   Do you worry about money? Do you worry about having enough money to buy the right clothes? Do some people care more about what you look like than who you are? Hudson Taylor had a refreshing approach to money. He trusted God. He knew that God would supply all his needs. Do you think you could try that? Hudson Taylor also believed that he should give as much money as possible to God. Can you think of different ways of doing this? If you don't have a lot of money - what other things can you give to God instead? Remember that God looks on the heart and doesn't care whether you are dressed in rags or riches. Look at these verses to see what God says about money, clothes etc: 1 Samuel 16:7; Matthew 6:25-34.

4   Hudson and Maria fell hopelessly in love. What do you think love is? Was it love for each other that kept Hudson and Maria going when their little girl died? Was it just that they were very strong people? Look up the following verse. Romans 5:8. What does this verse tell you about love? Read this verse too 1 Peter 5:7. Isn't it great that God cares for us? Whatever happens we know that his love never fails. Psalm 13:5.

5   Hudson Taylor had what a lot of people might call a very sad life. He was sick as a child, the first woman he loved didn't want to marry him, in the end his little girl and his wife died. Has someone close to you ever died? How did it make you feel? Did you know that God knows how this feels? God's Son Jesus Christ died on the cross. If death frightens you, you should speak to God about it. He understands us and can help us. We can talk to God about anything at all. Read the following verses which talk about death. Psalm 23:4; Psalm 116:8; Proverbs 14:32; Romans 4:25; Romans 8:38-39; Romans 15:54-58

6   At the end of this book we read the story of a girl called Lauren. Is she what you imagine a typical missionary to be? Do you have to go to another country to be a missionary or be a certain age? What does God say about mission? Read Mark 16:15-16. What are the consequences for someone who does not hear and believe the Gospel of Jesus Christ? If you love God and believe that Jesus Christ died to give you forgiveness of sins - then you too can be a missionary. In fact - if you love God - you don't have a choice. You've just got to tell others about how amazing he is. God has told you to do this and he means what he says! Think about how you can do this today!

Hudson Taylor Quotes

'When will it dawn on the Lord's people
that God's command to preach the gospel
to every creature was not intended for the
waste-paper basket?'
Hudson Taylor

'You do not need a great faith, but faith in a
great God.'
Hudson Taylor

'There is a God; he has spoken to us
in the Bible;
he means what he says.'
Hudson Taylor

'Is our path dark? God is our sun.
Are we in danger? God is our shield.'
Hudson Taylor

'I have not known what anxiety is since the Lord taught me that the work is his. My great business in life is to please God. Walking with him in the light, I never feel a burden.'
Hudson Taylor

' When I cannot read; when I cannot think; when I cannot even pray; I can trust'
Hudson Taylor

'Hudson Taylor prayed as if everything depended on the praying and worked as if everything depended on the working.'
Howard Taylor

Trailblazers

A Voice In The Dark
Richard Wurmbrand

by
Catherine Mackenzie

'Where am I? What are you doing? Where are you taking me?' Richard's voice cracked under the strain. His heart was pounding so hard he could hardly breathe. Gasping for air he realized - this was the nightmare! Thoughts came so quickly he could hardly make sense of anything. 'I must keep control,' he said out loud. An evil chuckle broke out from beside him. 'You are no longer in control. We are your worst nightmare!'...

When Richard Wurmbrand is arrested, imprisoned and tortured, he finds himself in utter darkness. Yet the people who put him there discover that their prisoner has a light which can still be seen in the dark - the love of God. This incredible story of one man's faith, despite horrific persecution, is unforgettable and will be an inspiration to all who read it.

ISBN 1-85792-298-0

The Freedom Fighter
William Wilberforce

by
Derick Bingham

'No! No!' cried the little boy, 'Please no! I want to stay with my mother!'
'Be quiet!' shouted the man who roughly pulled his mother from him. She was taken to a raised platform and offered for sale, immediately. The heart-broken mother was to be separated from her little boy for the rest of her life...

This was the fate of thousands of women and children in the days before slavery was abolished. One man fought to bring freedom and relief from the terrors of the slave trade; it took him forty-five years. His name was William Wilberforce. His exciting story shows the amazing effect his faith in Christ and his love for people had on transforming a nation.

'A story deserving to be told to a new generation.'
The Prime Minister the Rt. Hon. Tony Blair, M.P.

ISBN 1-85792-371-5

From Wales to Westminster
Martyn Lloyd-Jones

by his grand-son
Christopher Catherwood

'Fire! Fire! - A woman shouted frantically. However, as the villagers desperately organised fire fighting equipment the Lloyd-Jones family slept. They were blissfully ignorant that their family home and livelihood was just about to go up in smoke. Martyn, aged ten, was snug in his bed, but his life was in danger.

What happened to Martyn? Who rescued him? How did the fire affect him and his family? And why is somebody writing a book about Martyn in the first place? In this book Christopher Catherwood, Martyn's grandson, tells you about the amazing life of his grandfather, Dr. Martyn Lloyd Jones. Find out about the young boy who trained to be a doctor at just sixteen years old. Meet the young man who was destined to become the Queen's surgeon and find out why he gave it all up to work for God. Read about Martyn Lloyd-Jones. He was enthusiastic and on fire for God. You will be, too, by the end of this book!

ISBN 1-85792-349-9

The Watch-maker's Daughter
Corrie Ten Boom

by
Jean Watson

If you like stories of adventure, courage and faith
- then here's one you won't forget. Corrie loved to
help others, especially handicapped children.
But her happy lifestyle in Holland is shattered
when he is sent to a Nazi concentration camp.
She suffered hardship and punishment but experienced God's love and help in unbearable situa-
tions.
Her amazing story has been told worldwide and
has inspired many people. Discover about one
of the most outstanding Christian women of the
20th century

ISBN 1-85792-116-X

LOOK OUT

FOR THE

FOLLOWING

NEW

TRAILBLAZERS

C S LEWIS
~The storyteller~
by Derick Bingham

GEORGE MULLER
~The Children's Champion~
by Irene Howatt

Look out for our

New Fiction Titles

Something to Shout About - Sheila Jacobs
Jane gets involved in a 'Save our Church' campaign but finds out that you can worship God anytime, anywhere.

Twice Freed - Patricia St. John
Onesimus is a slave in Philemon's household. All he has ever wanted is to live his life in freedom. He wants nothing to do with Jesus Christ or the man, Paul, who preaches about him. One day Onesimus steals some money from his master. Find out what happens and if Onesimus realises the meaning of true freedom!

Martin's Last Chance - Heidi Schmidt
Rebekka and Martin live in Germany. They are firm friends and hang out everywhere together. Martin has a rare heart and lung disorder and is waiting for his last chance to get a transplant. See how Martin trust's God throughout his illness. Find out how he and Rebekka cope with the school bullies and how Rebekka finds out for herself who God is and what he is all about.

CHRISTIAN FOCUS

Good books with the real message of hope!

Christian Focus Publications publishes biblically-accurate books for adults and children.

If you are looking for quality bible teaching for children then we have a wide and excellent range of bible story books - from board books to teenage fiction, we have it covered.

You can also try our new Bible teaching Syllabus for 3-9 year olds and teaching materials for pre-school children.

These children's books are bright, fun and full of biblical truth, an ideal way to help children discover Jesus Christ for themselves. Our aim is to help children find out about God and get them enthusiastic about reading the Bible, now and later in their life.

Find us at our web page:
www.christianfocus.com